PRIVATE VIRTUE
AND
PUBLIC POLICY

PRIVATE VIRTUE
AND
PUBLIC POLICY

Catholic Thought and National Life

Edited by

James Finn

Transaction Publishers
New Brunswick (U.S.A.) and London (U.K.)

BX
1795
.E27
P75
1990
155246
Mar. 1992

Library of Congress Catalog Number: 89-30457
ISBN: 0–88738–306–8
Printed in the United States of America

Library of Congress Cataloging-in-Publication Data

Private virtue and public policy : Catholic thought and national life
   / edited by James Finn.
       p.   cm.
     Includes index.
     ISBN 0-88738-306-8
       1. Economics—Religious aspects—Catholic Church.
   2. Sociology, Christian (Catholic)   3. United States—Economic
   conditions—1945–
   4. Catholic Church. National Conference of Catholic Bishops.
   Economic justice for all.   5. Lay Commission on Catholic Social
   Teaching and the U.S. Economy.   6. Catholic Church—Doctrines.
   I. Finn, James, 1924–
   BX1795.E27P75   1989
   261.8′5′0973—dc20   89-30457
                                                                    CIP

Contents

Introduction

James Finn

The following essays form part of an ongoing dialogue on economic justice with the Catholic bishops of the United States. Although many people have contributed to that dialogue—American Catholics, Americans who are not Catholics, Catholics who are not American, and those who are neither—a special word needs to be said about the principal contributor to and inspirer of this volume: the Lay Commission on Catholic Social Teaching and the U.S. Economy. Under the general guidance of William E. Simon and Michael Novak, who served as chairman and vice chairman respectively, the small group of laypeople who formed the commission decided early on to issue a report that would roughly parallel that of the American bishops. It would, that is, address itself to the same subject and draw upon the same rich resources of Catholic social thought and the American experience. The commission's statement, *Toward the Future,* which appeared shortly before the first draft of the bishops' report, remains the principal document produced by the Lay Commission. (That small volume continues to be circulated in English and other languages, and has proved to be quite persuasive.)

After the bishops published the first draft of *Economic Justice for All: Catholic Social Teaching and the U.S. Economy* in November 1984 they modified and, in a number of ways, improved their report. As a very interested and active participant in the dialogue that the bishops explicitly invited, the Lay Commission issued its critical commentary, based on the bishops' third draft, from which the final text, approved in June 1986, differs very little. That commentary, "Liberty and Justice for All," by Simon and Novak is included here with additional essays on discrete aspects of economic justice that the bishops examined—or failed to examine. For, as more than one of these essays explicitly states, issues of economic justice must be discussed in more than economic terms. (It is no accident that this volume stresses, in different contexts, the relation between private virtue and public policy.)

Since both the bishops and the members of the Lay Commission are joined as Americans within the Catholic communion, and since both considered economic justice within the context of Catholic social thought and the American experience, it should not be surprising that they are in close agreement on many fundamental issues. Each group emphasizes, for example, the dignity of the human person as fundamental to sound economic life, and the treatment of the poor as a litmus test for the moral quality of a society. But neither should it be surprising that there are also significant differences and that, as in many familial exchanges, they sometimes have a sharp edge. When such differences arise, it is well that they be made as clearly and precisely as possible. As the noted theologian John Courtney Murray, S.J., observed some years ago, real disagreement—as distinguished from simply opposing attitudes and opinions—is an achievement. It presupposes that each party truly understands what the other is saying. Only when both parties know and acknowledge where they disagree is any advance in the dialogue possible.

Against those who say that economics and morality have nothing in common, that they exist in separate, impermeable compartments, the bishops strongly oppose themselves and the full weight of Catholic social teaching. This initial premise meets with strong resistance in many sectors of our society, and its spirited assertion by the bishops deserves equally spirited support. They correctly point out that any economic system is the work of people, not nature. As such it is subject to change by people with particular goals in mind. The bishops then proceed to enumerate a number of both general and highly specific goals toward which they believe our economic policies should be directed. They also specify a number of particular policies that they think can best realize those goals.

Although the goals the bishops set forth can, indeed, be described in economic terms and must be realized within our economic structures, whether they should be sought and how they should be sought must be decided in terms of our political economy. In the determination of economic goods and the allocation of economic resources, choices must be made. Whether they are best made by the private sector or the government, and by which agencies in each, are, in the broadest sense, political decisions. Our citizens and their political representatives will say Yes to this proposal and No to that. Since not all citizens will make the same judgments, the decisions will inevitably be divisive. They will divide one group from another.

The choices will be made on the basis of whether the proposals appear to be feasible or not, but, even more important, on whether they are desirable or not. Those decisions will rest, ultimately, on those values that most profoundly inform our culture, on our understanding of the person, the human community, and the relations of both to the transcendent. The progression of dependency runs, succinctly but not simply, from economics to politics, from politics to culture, from culture to morality/religion. Not simply, because this is not entirely a one-way street; one set of values influences another, economic and political decisions, for example, having the power to modify and shape even long-standing societal values and habits of behavior.

But in considering the relation of morality to the political and economic dimensions of our society, the primary claim that the bishops have to our attention is not that they are good economists (though some of them may be) or that they are good political analysts (though some of them may be) but that by virtue of their office and training they are empowered to speak to the nature, and needs, and the destiny of the person and the human community. As they themselves say, the area of their expertise is religion and morality. Given this understanding one can more readily grasp why the bishops stated that not all of their statements should be accorded equal moral authority, and also why the more nearly technical and specific their recommendations became the more they exposed themselves to competing judgments and criticism.

Any full assessment of the bishops' Pastoral Letter, from the most sympathetic to the most skeptical, must attempt to answer fundamental questions. Given the bishops' stated purpose:

1. What did they do, and how well?
2. What, if anything significant, did they fail to do?
3. What does it matter?

Collectively, the following essays address these questions, both explicitly and implicitly. Although no single volume can exhaust all that is to be said on the many particular issues raised in the Pastoral Letter, it is possible to indicate particular strengths of the bishops' achievement, to offer evidence and analyses that lead to conclusions different from theirs, to indicate valuable approaches that they failed to explore, and to push to greater intellectual precision crucial terms whose content has been assumed rather than cogently developed. The conscientious reader of this book will understand how experts in various fields can consider many of these issues and arrive at judgments that are sometimes close to those of the bishops and sometimes at considerable variance from them.

On the basis of past participation in the ongoing dialogue on the American economy and Catholic social teaching, I do not presume that all who read this book will accept its findings when they run counter to those of the bishops. But the warm reception given to *Toward the Future* indicates that many will. And this fact underlines a significant feature of the bishops' letter: given the approach they took and the high degree of specificity of many of their recommendations, their letter is necessarily, inevitably divisive. But across the divide thus created, the dialogue must continue. The reader who takes that letter and this volume together will be better prepared to participate vigorously and usefully in that dialogue.

1

Liberty and Justice for All

William E. Simon and Michael Novak

This Lay Commission has studied the final draft of the U.S. Catholic bishops' letter, *Economic Justice for All: Catholic Social Teaching and the U.S. Economy* (June 1986). We commend our bishops for the improvements introduced since their first draft (November 1984). In our earlier report, *Toward the Future,* issued before the bishops' first draft, we raised many of the same questions as the bishops later did. We have been gratified to see how many of the points we raised –particularly concerning the family—have found their way into the bishops' final draft. We commend the bishops for being attentive to their many critics.

The bishops also released a second, related document—a short, twenty-nine-paragraph "Pastoral Message on Economic Justice for All"—intended to accompany the longer, discursive draft as a sort of summary for pastoral use. We highly admire this short "Pastoral Message." Thus our comments below are directed entirely to the long third draft of the Pastoral Letter released in June. We do not address the short message (except for its brief misstatement of papal teaching on economic rights in paragraph 17, to be discussed below). On the contrary, we find its tone and balance, its nonpartisanship and moral transcendence far superior to the formulations about some of the passages in the latter, while the short "Pastoral Message" represents in our eyes the ideal we wish the longer version had met.

Again the bishops have invited all Americans to continue this debate upon economic realities and, in response, we again make public our own reflections. First, we emphasize the positive. Second, we list several serious flaws still to be found in the long final draft.

General Comments

We think it admirable that our bishops placed stress on lifting the poor out of poverty. That is precisely what the Statue of Liberty ("Send me your tired, your poor . . .") symbolizes. And lifting up the poor is precisely what, generation after generation, the United States has done—and is still doing. All American families, like those first Catholic families that arrived on the *Ark* and the *Dove*, have benefited from this national policy.

Lifting the poor out of poverty has also been one of the main pillars of U.S. international policy, at least since Franklin D. Roosevelt and Harry S. Truman articulated the "Four Freedoms." Lifting up the poor is one of the three liberations for which the liberal society has always stood: (1) *liberation from tyranny and from torture,* through democracy; (2) *liberation from oppression of conscience, information, and ideas,* through free churches, the free press, free intellectual life, and institutional pluralism; and (3) *liberation from poverty,* through capitalist institutions such as private property, markets, enterprise, invention, and free associations.

While we commend their good intentions, we have serious concerns that practical recommendations made by the bishops to help the poor of the Third World will end up causing greater poverty and misery. Economic policies are judged by their results.

We do not count ourselves among those who think that, in speaking of economics, the bishops are overstepping their proper authority. On the contrary, we take pride in Catholic social teaching. We welcome the bishops' constructive contributions to that unfinished tradition, even though lay Catholics also have a primary calling to contribute to that tradition.

In some ways, the final draft includes stronger statements in favor of a capitalist economy, such as that of the United States, than are to be found in any other document of the tradition of Catholic social thought. They have mentioned the crucial role of creativity and invention, the role of enterprise, the importance of economic growth and job creation and other institutions of the free society. For this we commend them.

In a few places, we fear that the bishops have neglected or obscured basic practical points, and have exhibited several practical confusions that are likely to lead to results that they do not intend. We also have some concern that the bishops have in a few places gone beyond the bounds of their authority in two respects. First, in some passages they have risked making prescriptions that belong more properly to lay authorities and public democratic choice. They thus risk cloaking their political and social opinions on concrete matters with ecclesiastical authority. Second, in some passages they have risked placing their moral authority behind practical economic policies whose unintended consequences, if errant and evil, can bring their genuine religious authority into disrepute. To the extent that they take sides in partisan issues, in matters not specifically entrusted to their care, they forfeit the moral authority of a position beyond partisan politics. Large sections of the final draft are properly sheltered from these faults. But no one can deny—either those who applaud or those who object—that some passages are both excessively concrete and excessively opinionated.

In the short "Pastoral Message" mentioned above, for example, the bishops clearly state that their long final draft goes into specifics and into concrete applications, not in order to insist that theirs is the only or the correct interpretation, but in order to "give an example" of how to move from general principles to concrete judgments. They write that they expect persons of good will to disagree about such matters, and they encourage them to do so. We accept this invitation to disagree. We are also constrained to say that the final draft's way of reasoning from general principles to concrete judgments does not set a good example. The final draft includes many hidden and partisan "middle axioms," ideas that mediate between general principles and matters of fact. The short "Pastoral Message" states clearly that the bishops do not intend to be ideological. But in bridging general principles with specific applications, the reasoning of the final draft is in places unmistakably ideological. It is far more so, apparently, than the bishops intended to be. This is, of course, most obvious to those who do not share that ideology.

A great many of the deficiencies that concern us are to be found in chapter 3 of their letter, "Selected Economic Policy Issues." Others are to be found in chapter 2, section B, "Ethical Norms for Economic Life" and in chapter 4, "A New American Experiment." These areas, in particular, belong especially to the vocation of laypersons. On these temporal matters, we judge that laypersons have specific responsibilities to accept the invitation by our bishops to enter fully into the national debate.

We share with our bishops the full intention of raising up every single poor person on earth from the tyranny of poverty. The dream of democratic and capitalist societies such as our own will not be fulfilled until there is a solid economic base placed under every single person on this planet, and until the reality of "liberty and justice for all" rings out around this planet from every sea to every shining sea.

We fear, though, that in this universal vision the bishops underestimate the role of liberty. Even the title of their letter, *Economic Justice for All,* leaves out the crucial element of social justice, namely liberty. Liberty is the ground of responsibility, and hence of human dignity. "Liberty"—in its distinctive American meaning of "liberty under law" and "under God"—is the distinctive American gift to the social teaching of the church. Indeed, the ideal of liberty now belongs to the vision of all peoples everywhere. Today, in both the socialist and the traditionalist world, more and more nations are grasping the central role of political liberty, and moving toward democracy; of freedom of conscience, inquiry, and speech, and moving toward "openness"; and of free economic institutions, and moving toward free economic activism, property rights, markets, incentives, and invention.

In deemphasizing liberty—preferring "solidarity"—we think the U.S. bishops have missed a precious historical opportunity. They have misread "the signs of the times." In this respect, we believe that the Vatican Instruction on "Christian Freedom and Liberation" has been more penetrating than the bishops' final draft.

Nonetheless, we praise the U.S. Catholic bishops both for opening up this crucial argument of our times and for proceeding in an open way, inviting us, and all who disagree with their own analysis

in its various parts, to enter openly into public debate in charity
and in civility.

The Catholic bishops of the United States affirmed at the Third
Council of Baltimore (1884) that the founders of the United States,
under Providence, "built better than they knew." The Catholic
bishops of the present generation have now opened up questions
larger and deeper than they themselves have plumbed. They have
invited all citizens to go beyond their own final draft. Forming our
own free association—in a distinctively American fashion—the
members of our Lay Commission gladly accept this challenge. We
thank our bishops for encouraging our work.

Serious Faults in the Bishops' Final Draft

Despite the many improvements that the bishops made in their
letter since 1984, we still find in the final draft several serious
intellectual defects. Among these are: (1) a failure to grasp what
makes poor nations into developed nations; (2) deficient under-
standings of *political economy* (the relative roles of government
and the free economy); (3) excessive trust in the state and its
officials; (4) an inadequate grasp of crucial concepts such as enterprise, markets, and profits; (5) significant confusions about economic rights; (6) fateful confusions between defense spending and
spending on weapons; (7) a preference for "solidarity" over pluralism; (8) an inadequate exposition of "liberty." Because of such
deficiencies, the final draft fails to grasp the distinctive nature of
the American experiment in political economy. Its descriptions of
poverty, welfare, unemployment, and taxation in the United States
remain significantly one-sided. And the final draft still remains blind
to moral and spiritual resources available in American economic
habits and institutions, thus failing to give the moral guidance that
many citizens long for.

We hope and pray that in a future effort the bishops will go more
deeply into these themes, and not cut short a flawed beginning. We
also hope and pray that they will instruct teachers in Catholic
schools, pastors, and others to be open to the full range of debate
upon these issues, guarding themselves faithfully against partisan
or one-sided treatment of important dimensions of reality. We do
not argue that there is only one set of reasonable views upon these

much-disputed issues. We do hold, with the bishops, that full pluralism and openness of discussion should prevail.

We note with regret that the avoidance of partisanship did not always mark the dissemination of their earlier Pastoral Letter on nuclear arms. We hope that on this issue the dissemination process will go much better, in fuller pluralism and nonpartisan inquiry.

We turn now to areas in which, in our judgment, the final draft falls short.

1. Raising up the Poor in the Third World

The letter of the U.S. bishops is being studied closely by Catholic bishops in the Third World. In Latin America, in Africa, in the Philippines, in South Korea, and in other nations in Asia, the Catholic people represent a significant cultural force. The economy in most such places is still characterized by residual practices of the feudal era, traditional ways of thinking, and precapitalist institutions. Very few facilities exist for empowering the poor: enabling them to incorporate small businesses, to avail themselves of credit, and to enter markets freely. Many markets are restricted through public licenses available only to the privileged and the well established, and the poor are in many effective ways prevented from engaging in economic activism.

Consider Latin America. Throughout that resource-rich continent, there are between 60 and 70 million young persons, already born, under the age of fifteen. Every year between now and the year 2000, these youngsters will begin entering the job market. Already facing massive unemployment and underemployment, Latin America will have to create between 60 and 70 million additional new jobs in order to employ these youngsters. How will these jobs be created? It seems unlikely that, by the year 2000, a higher number of persons will be employed in agriculture. Neither large domestic corporations nor transnationals are likely to be able to employ more than a tiny fraction of the unemployed. Clearly, Latin America needs 10 to 15 million new small businesses, both industrial and commercial, each hiring five to ten persons, to absorb this massive labor force. But how will these new enterprises be created?

In most nations, the process of incorporating and licensing new businesses is lengthy and very costly. The law favors the already privileged. Law, custom, and the prevailing cultural ethos are in many places hostile to enterprise. This is a massive roadblock to the economic aspirations of the poor.

Experience shows that God gives abundant economic talents to the poor, and that, where the law and institutions favor enterprise, the poor can in massive numbers and in a short time exit from poverty, through the use of their God-given talents. Each person, Christians believe, is made in the image of the Creator. Each is capable of economic creativity. Thus nations such as Japan, South Korea, Hong Kong, Taiwan, and Singapore have grown spectacularly from the ravages of World War II, multiplying their per-capita income ten to fifteen times during a single generation. The Pastoral Letter of the U.S. bishops fails both to point out these universal possibilities and to encourage the necessary institutional reforms.

In practical terms, the Pastoral Letter offers the poor of the Third World very little hope. The Pastoral Letter emphasizes foreign aid, without pointing out that foreign aid often helps the poor very little, is often mishandled by elites, and does little to empower the poorest. It also fails to point out that if the billions of dollars already expended in aid—and the further hundreds of billions of dollars expended in loans—can be misused by elites, then the future promise of further aid is not really very hopeful. In many developing countries, basic institutional changes are needed. Without these basic institutional changes, designed to empower the poor at the bottom of the ladder to become economic activists, the prognosis for the future is not bright. Yet there are many examples in the developing world of peoples that have made spectacular economic progress in a short time. These examples are ignored in the final draft.

This is all the more surprising since most of the economically successful developing nations are pluralistically adapting to their own conditions institutions pioneered in the development of the United States. Except for such institutions, the United States today might be as poor as Brazil, Africa, or Asia. Great deposits of natural resources are not sufficient to move a nation to development. Among the institutions crucial for the early development of the United States were: Article I, section 8, of the U.S. Constitution, committing the nation to "promote the progress of science and useful arts'' through a patent office; the Homestead Act favoring a multiplicity of owners rather than a few large landholders; the land-grant colleges and the Extension Service; farm credit bureaus; local savings and loan institutions open to all; credit bureaus; cooperatives; assistance to small businesses; a massive commitment to universal education; a habit of association (''base communities'') and ease of incorporation. Without such institutions, the early economic development of the continental United States can scarcely be imagined.

In Japan, Hong Kong, South Korea, Taiwan, Singapore, and elsewhere today there are many examples of successful, rapid economic development, adapting pluralistically to each culture parallel developmental institutions. For examples of success, one need not point only to the United States. Ideas pioneered in this country have proved to be immensely successful elsewhere when adapted to local conditions and customs supplemented by new techniques invented locally. What has characterized economic progress in all of these nations is a vibrant work ethic not eroded by governmental encouragement of dependency. This is a moral as well as an institutional factor.

The experience of the United States in moving from an undeveloped to a developed nation is, therefore, not without significance elsewhere. But the bishops' final draft gives the founders of the United States credit mainly for their experiment in political and civil rights, while failing to grasp the true originality of the American experiment in economic liberty. The founders of our nation launched a ''commercial republic,'' an experiment in political *economy*. The economic originality of the American model has been at least as decisive in history as its political originality. The final draft fails to grasp the crucial economic insights of the American experiment.

2. A Preferential Option for the State

The final draft can by no means be called a socialist document. It guards against a purely statist approach to helping the poor. It is, clearly, a pro-capitalist document. Nonetheless, again and again, the final draft turns to the state to ''direct'' economic activism, to create jobs, to play a determining role in foreign-aid assistance, and the like. The Lay Commission agrees that, in political economy, the political system plays a significant—but not central—role. That role, in our judgment, is best described as empowering people. The state ought to permit economic activity to be open, free, legally accessible to all, easy to enter, broadly supported in law. The state ought to reduce barriers preventing the poor and underprivileged from entering markets, exercising their God-given talents, finding ample opportunity to dream their own dreams, and putting their own vision into reality. The state must be active, but excessive state entanglement raises barriers.

To repeat, we are not opposed to an activist state, but wise activism means counting costs as well as benefits. A wise citizenry properly hunts out government programs and activities that erect barriers to, and introduce biases against, productive activity. For example, minimum-wage laws can restrict economic activism and hold down the number of employed. Welfare programs giving direct payments to individuals may, among their effects, subsidize non-participation, raise the cost of working against the cost of not working, raise the cost of employing people, and alter the sense of social responsibility and personal dignity. An unwise tax system may penalize saving and productivity-advancing activities. Actions by the state, while called for by the conception of *political economy* and often necessary, are not ipso facto good. They must be constantly under review and subject to reform.

Throughout the final draft, by contrast, there is a more sympathetic understanding of political activism than of economic activism. Yet it is chiefly the latter that is the engine of economic development. Economic development begins from the bottom up, through empowering the poor, not from the top down through extending political privileges.

To be sure, the final draft takes pains at several places to extol the role of mediating institutions and of social vitalities independent of the state. We applaud such passages. Still, the secret to economic development lies in the economic activism of the poor—in ease of incorporation, in the accessibility of commercial licenses, in the availability of local credit, and in an ethos and legal climate favorable to the talents of the poor. Even a few paragraphs highlighting the centrality of the economic activism of the poor would have dramatic effects in the efforts of the church worldwide to empower the poor, through institutions designed to shake the grip of the privileged upon economic life in most Third World countries.

3. Dim Light on Enterprise, Markets, and Profits

The final draft speaks far too briefly about enterprise, spends more time attacking the straw man of "unfettered markets" than in grasping the importance to the poor of easy and rapid entry into markets, and describes profits as "a vexing problem."

In fact, "profit" is another word for development. It is achieved by those things that produce development: enterprise, risk-taking, mobilizing saving and directing it into productive uses. If an economic system is drawing no more income out of economic activities than will cover costs, there is *no* development, only stagnation. The profit motive is a social discipline, measuring whether genuine economic development is being made or not. One of profit's disciplining effects is to direct capital and other resources into their most creative uses. Economic development is not everything, but for the poor it is crucially important. A stagnant or declining economy offers the poor little hope indeed. That profits should be used wisely and for the common good is an obvious and important moral principle. But without profits, there is no development. Neither the profit motive nor the effort to achieve development is "a vexing problem." Both are absolutely crucial to the welfare of the poor.

Further, markets cannot exist without commonly accepted rules, regulations, and ethical disciplines. In a crucial sense, there can be no such thing as an "unfettered" market. In the real world, in most traditional countries, the problem is that markets are skewed in favor of the traditionally privileged. Only the privileged can obtain papers of incorporation, licenses, and credit. Market entry is restricted. The poor are effectively excluded. The idea of "free market" means, not the absence of legal regulation or ethical standards but, rather, equal opportunity, open entry, and the legal and institutional support for universal access among all citizens. Where in Latin America, Africa, or Asia are there "unfettered markets" open to the poor? In few places, indeed. It is one of the chief roles of government in the political economy of democratic capitalism to keep markets open to all. Behind this role lies the fundamental principle: the cause of the wealth of nations is the wit, invention, discovery, and enterprise exercised through economic activism. When one speaks of "free markets," one does not mean there are no interventions from the political system. Rather, one means such interventions are prudent and confined to cases in which markets are failing or in which market performance can be improved. Finally, enterprise is not the same as entrepreneurship. Enterprise is a talent and a virtue, a habit of discovering unmet needs and of inventing goods and services not previously available, and a determination to provide goods and services at better prices or with better quality than offered elsewhere. Entrepreneurship arises from the habit of enterprise but adds to it the practical skills involved in actually realizing new ideas. The person of enterprise has the habit of inventing new ideas. The entrepreneur has the further habit of realizing new ideas under the conditions of ambiguity and contingency prevailing in the real world of fact.

To its credit, the final draft does praise enterprise. But considering the crucial importance of enterprise, the final draft is surprisingly silent about its characteristics, its preconditions, and the methods of encouraging its frequent appearance. Talents of enterprise are widely diffused among the poor. The practical skills necessary to their flowering can be identified. Supporting institutions can be constructed. Among these are institutions permitting rapid and cheap incorporation; protecting patents and copyrights; and laws favoring capital formation and realistic depreciation schedules, and so forth.

4. Economic Rights

The final draft (nos. 78–83) much improved beyond the first draft upon this point, still does not properly report the papal teaching upon economic rights. In *Pacem in Terris,* Pope John XXIII clearly distinguished "economic rights" (nos. 18–22) from "the right to life and a worthy manner of living" (no. 11). Economic rights in papal thought include rights to initiative, to physically and morally healthful working conditions (with special rights for wives, mothers, and all women), to opportunity to achieve responsibilities compatible with talents, to work that provides a decent standard of living for one's family, and to private property and its inherent social duties. Economic rights in papal thought protect the activism of ordinary people, protect families from dependency upon the state, and are consistent with the economic rights carefully defended in the U.S. intellectual traditions. In both, rights to economic liberties are protected, as well as rights to civil liberties.

In papal thought, such "economic rights" are treated quite separately from "welfare rights." Even the word "rights" appears to have a different meaning in these two separate contexts. Thus, for Pope John XXIII, the rights to life include such "welfare rights" as the rights "to means which are necessary and suitable to the proper development of life," including "the right to security in cases of sickness, inability to work, widowhood, old age, unemployment, or any other case in which he is deprived of the means of subsistence *through no fault of his own* (*Pacem in Terris,* no. 11; italics added). In other words, the individual has the duty to be self-reliant. "[H]e who possesses certain rights has likewise the duty to claim those rights as marks of his dignity, . . ." (ibid., no. 44). But when *through no fault of his own,* one cannot meet essential needs of life, the individual has a right, because of his or her humanity, to help from society. This help is not necessarily to come from the state, but rather, from the state only as a last resort, through a social "safety net."

In papal teaching, "economic rights" protect citizens in their *activism* and in their *active* contributions to society. By contrast, "welfare rights" protect those citizens unable to be active, in their need to receive benefits. The latter need arises only from the inability of some citizens, through no fault of their own, to be self-reliant. Self-reliance is the ideal of papal thought. To protect the truly needy, welfare programs are necessary in any good society. To protect liberty and autonomy, welfare dependency is to be discouraged. That is why "welfare rights" must be treated with caution. As the final draft does observe, Catholic social teaching emphasizes responsibilities as well as rights.

Further, in our highly legalistic society, it is dangerous to speak of rights without exact clarity. Papal teaching does not speak of "constitutional rights" or "legal rights." It has in mind "rights" binding upon other human beings morally. The institutional mechanisms through which such moral obligations are to be fulfilled are left to each society to work out. Such moral obligations must be met; on that there is unanimity. Still, there are grave dangers in confusing moral rights with constitutional or legal rights.

In the highly legalistic American context, loose speech about "rights" invites massive legal entanglements. If the state were to become paternalistic, it would become (as Tocqueville warned) "a new soft despotism" dangerous to liberty, to self-reliance, to initiative, and to moral autonomy. Theories that loosely invite the intrusion of the state, however benign their intentions, invite this soft tyranny. The state obliged to provide for the daily welfare of all its citizens gains over them exquisite control.

Experience shows that many forms of welfare are more efficiently and more morally provided by other agents than the state. While welfare programs by the state are sometimes necessary, they typically suffer from three defects: they operate by coercion, by abstract regulation, and by impersonal methods; they often encourage dependency and discourage personal responsibility; and what they take coercively and efficiently from some they provide without any sense of human contact or human concern to unknown others with unknown effects.

We are very much in favor of a disciplined and realistic welfare state that, while encouraging independence and self-reliance, provides assistance to those who cannot rely on themselves. As we wrote in *Toward the Future,* "One measure of a good society is how well it cares for the weakest and most vulnerable of its members." In our view, the best intellectual defense of the welfare state scrupulously limits the language of "economic rights" to the rights of activist individuals and their associations. (These include the papally approved "economic rights" to initiative, responsibility, private property, etc.) Such a theory carefully places welfare "rights" in the context of duties of self-reliance, and ascribes them only to those persons unable *through no fault of their own* to fulfill these duties. In addition, such a theory turns to empirical research in order to discern the most effective means for providing welfare benefits that strengthen habits of self-reliance and personal autonomy. Such a theory notes, with Pope John Paul II, that among those able to work, human dignity is rooted in work. Several passages in the final draft commendably recognize this point.

Thus we note with regret that—just as we feared—the misstatement of papal teaching in the long draft of June 1986 leads directly to an even balder misstatement in the short "Pastoral Message" of October 1986. In paragraph 17 of the latter, the bishops write: "As John XXIII declared, all people have a right to life, food, clothing, shelter, rest, medical care, education, and employment." But again, Pope John XXIII does *not* assert this of "all people." He asserts it only of those who are unable *"through no fault of [their] own"* to meet their responsibilities to provide for themselves and their dependents (*Pacem in Terris,* no. 11; italics added). Able persons have the *duty* to be self-reliant. They do not have a "right" to be dependent, unless circumstances beyond their control prevent them from taking responsibility for their own needs. In the same paragraph 17 of the bishops' message, "economic rights" are not properly distinguished from "welfare rights," as John XXIII did distinguish them (compare *Pacem in Terris,* nos. 18–22 with no. 11). Further, the different meaning of the word "rights" in the two different phrases, "economic rights" and "welfare rights," is not observed; the second meaning is conditional. This lapse strengthens our view that errors in the June draft may have unintended effects in the process of dissemination. The latter will have to be very closely watched.

5. *Defense Spending vs. Spending on Arms*

More than once, in opposition to current levels of U.S. spending on defense, the final draft confuses the entire defense budget with spending on weapons. Five crucial facts are omitted.

a. Defense spending includes salaries, pensions, family allowances, the costs of installations and transport, recruiting and training costs, communications, and other fixed costs. The United States has no draft and relies upon volunteers. Its total armed forces in 1985 numbered 2.2 million (approximately 2 percent of its total 109 million civilian employees). Current defense spending in 1985 (at $245 billion), represented 6.4 percent of gross national product (GNP) and 26 percent of the federal budget. This already represents a large decline from 9 percent of GNP and 52 percent of the federal budget in 1960. An investment of 6.4 percent of GNP in the defense of priceless liberty hardly seems excessive.

b. Actual spending on *procurement,* including weapons, equipment, communications gear, and the like, in 1985 totaled $70 billion, or 29 percent of the total defense budget, about 2 percent of GNP and about 7 percent of the federal budget. Two considerations must be taken into account. Since weapons both wear out and become obsolete, and must be replaced in cycles averaging about fifteen years, spending on arms goes in cycles. There are low years (as during the 1970s) and high years (during the 1980s). But even in the highest years, spending on arms represents only a very small investment in the future of liberty. Second, it would seem to be as imprudent to spend too little as to spend too much, and the measure of prudence is need. In a democracy, the people must weigh that need in the light of world events. In our own view, because of the imbalance created by vast Soviet spending during the 1970s, our own nation is erring dangerously on the side of an inadequate deterrent. Sufficiency to deter is the minimal measure.

  c. In their Pastoral Letter on nuclear policy, the U.S. Catholic bishops urged the people of the United States to increase spending on conventional defense and to decrease spending on nuclear defense. But spending on conventional arms is currently almost five times higher than spending on nuclear arms. The latter is by far the least costly deterrent. Thus the Catholic bishops themselves seem to be in favor of higher defense spending. Their advice in the two pastorals is contradictory.

  d. It is true that the United States spends a higher proportion of GNP (about 6.4 percent) on all elements of defense spending than West Germany (about 4.3 percent) and Japan (less than 1 percent). This is because the United States has assumed heavy burdens for the defense both of Western Europe and of the free nations of Asia. It may be that the bishops want Western European nations and Japan to raise their own defense spending in order to defend themselves without the help of the United States; but this is unlikely—and it would be unwise and dangerous policy.

  e. The U.S.S.R. maintains military forces as the very center and linchpin of its economy, at between 14 and 16 percent of GNP. Soviet military forces defeated Hitler's Eastern armies in 1944, but are now far stronger than Hitler's military at the height of its power. Soviet naval and air forces now operate in every ocean, off the shores of the United States, Japan, Sweden, and the small band of other free nations of the planet. Soviet strategic nuclear forces are superior in several respects to the U.S. nuclear deterrent. Soviet strategic antiballistic missile defenses already in place are vast, whereas those of the United States exist only on the drawing boards. The danger of nuclear blackmail is high. If it was not moral for the free nations to show the face of weakness and disarmament to Adolf Hitler during the 1930s, why is it moral to disarm in the face of Soviet power today? Those who cried out "Peace! Peace!" during the 1930s did not deter war. On the contrary, they acquired responsibility for emboldening aggressors. On this point, Walter Lippmann came to regret bitterly his own behavior in the 1930s:

> I was too weak-minded to take a stand against the exorbitant folly of the Washington Disarmament Conference. In fact, I followed the fashion, and . . . celebrated the disaster as a triumph and denounced the admirals who dared to protest. Of that episode in my life I am ashamed, all the more so because I had no excuse for not knowing better.[1]

6. The Preference for "Solidarity" over "Pluralism"

Throughout the final draft, appeal is made to "solidarity," even where "cooperation" would better serve the argument, especially among a pluralistic people. "Solidarity" leaves scant room for dissent, disagreement, and the autonomy of conscience. In European languages, perhaps, "solidarity" may be rooted in experiences of cultural homogeneity. To the American ear, however, "solidarity" suggests solid ranks in lockstep. The American people are swift to cooperate—one person for his motives, another for hers—but they deeply cherish the dignity and liberty of conscience. They value dissent. They properly fear authoritarianism from any quarter. They recognize international obligations, human brotherhood, cooperation among the nations, and responsibilities beyond borders. In this sense, they recognize that all upon this planet are one family under God. But to describe this reality as "solidarity" rather than as "cooperation" offends their sense of liberty and diversity. E pluribus unum is the national motto, but its key lies as much in respect for diversity, pluralism, and freely given cooperation as in ultimate unity.

Unaccountably, the final draft hardly ever quotes from American sources—from Jefferson, Madison, Lincoln, Franklin Delano Roosevelt, John F. Kennedy; from Jonathan Edwards, Orestes Brownson, William James, Reinhold Niebuhr, John Courtney Murray; from the Third Plenary Council of Baltimore, Bishop Spalding, Archbishops Ireland, Hughes, Gibbons; or even from the writings of Alexis de Tocqueville, Edmund Burke, John Stuart Mill, and Lord Acton on America. Instead, most of the intellectual sources of the final draft are derived from the European or Latin American experience.

7. An Inadequate Exposition of "Liberty"

"Liberty," a highly equivocal word, is nonetheless central to the American experiment in politics, economics, and cultural pluralism. The history of its conceptualization, of the habits of the heart in which it is embodied, and of its institutional realization in the United States is quite different from its history in other cultures around the planet. In not a few countries of Europe, for example, liberty frequently means liberty *from* the law or *against* the law. By contrast, the liberty Americans cherish is liberty *under* the law and liberty *under* God. (This is why the Statue of Liberty carries a book or a tablet of the law in one hand, a torch signifying mind against darkness in the other, why liberty is symbolized by a woman and not a warrior, and why her face is serious, purposive, and resolute.) For Americans, "confirm thy soul in self-control" is a key to the expression "sweet land of liberty." No American hymn sings of a "sweet land of equality."

The equality Americans value lies in "equality before the law," under a regime "of laws, not of men." Such equality demands a broad range of diverse outcomes, consistent with the use each free person makes of his or her unique talents and common liberties.

By contrast, an underlying theme behind the final draft appears to be a vision, not of justice based on liberty, but of an equality of income and wealth. That concept of equality is incompatible with respect for liberty. It is also necessarily unfair, since individuals differ enormously both in talent and in effort; equal outcomes are accordingly unjust. James Madison pointed out in the *Federalist* that a regime of liberty depends upon a diversity of faculties for acquiring property, on the grounds that such diversity is always found among people. He resisted in the name of liberty all appeals to such envy as is destructive of both liberty and prosperity. Thus certain conceptions of equality are hostile to the American Constitution and to Catholic social thought. The final draft does not adequately explore the tension between equality and liberty.

It is not possible to give an adequate exposition of the U.S. economy without discussing the particular American understanding of liberty, and especially of economic liberties. In fact, the U.S. Constitution in many places devotes many lines precisely to the economic liberties reserved to American citizens. The powers of the federal government concerning economic liberties are specifically enumerated and limited. These limitations have been of no small consequence for the progress of the practical arts and practical sciences in this blessed land. Indeed, in Article I the government of the United States expressly committed itself to "promote the progress of science and useful arts" through granting to "authors and inventors" for a limited time "the right" to the fruit of their discoveries. James Madison (against Jefferson, who preferred prizes administered by government) expressly argued that a regime of personally directed liberty, attracted by incentives, would be more beneficial to unleashing a tide of invention and discovery. Thus the founders acted upon the hypothesis that the primary cause of the wealth of nations is progress in the arts and sciences, that is, invention and discovery. This is the only place in which the word "right" is used in the body of the original Constitution. It is a provision of immense and untold significance for economic development.

In brief, we are saddened that the final draft fails to grasp the conceptual and institutional originality of the U.S. experiment in economic development. To hold that the U.S. founders launched an experiment in political and civil rights only, as the final draft asserts, is historically inaccurate; the American experiment in economic rights (understood as in Pope John XXIII's *Pacem in Terris,* nos. 18–22) was of at least equal universal relevance. Indeed, it is difficult to imagine the subsequent economic development of contemporary West Germany, Japan, and even nineteenth-century England apart from lessons learned through the American experiment in economic rights. Scholars and statesmen from around the world have studied this economic experiment assiduously.

8. Inadequate Descriptions of Reality in the Contemporary United States

In describing poverty, income, wealth, taxation, and unemployment in the United States, the final draft omits many important facts and, on the whole, gives a one-sided and partial description of reality.

a. Poverty: In 1985 the official measure of poverty in the United States was virtually an $11,000 yearly income for a nonfarm family of four. To be grasped adequately by non-Americans, this standard must be translated into the currencies of their own nations. Whereas only 14 percent of U.S. citizens fall below this standard, far higher percentages fall below it in most nations of the world, even in Western Europe. This standard was derived by allowing an annual expenditure of $3,666 ($70 per week) for food, and multiplying that amount by three. Moreover, it counts pre-tax, cash income only, omitting the market value of such governmentally derived benefits as food stamps ($11 billion in 1985), housing assistance ($6 billion), medical care ($37 billion), free public education through the twelfth grade, and other benefits. If the total package of non-cash, means-tested benefits given to the poor by the U.S. federal government in 1985 ($56 billion) were divided among the nation's 7 million poor families, these benefits would average $8,000 per family. The non-means-tested benefits (Medicare for those over age sixty-five, e.g., goes to all, not only the poor) would take the total of federal benefits disbursed to individuals in 1985 to $127 billion. This does not include benefits paid by the states, localities, and private sources.

There are heart-rending problems among some of the poor in the United States. We have not yet designed optimal programs to assist them. But it is wrong to pass over in silence the fact that the generation of U.S. citizens since 1965 has authorized immense annual monetary outlays to help the poor.

In stating the percentage of the U.S. poor (14 percent), one must also take into account the noncash benefits given to the poor in 1985, benefits scarcely in existence in 1965. For the individuals represented by the statistics in 1985, "poverty" does not have the same meaning as it did before the funding of so many noncash benefits. Moreover, in counting income, the Census Bureau does not now take account of personally held assets or voluntary choice of a way of life. Not all who have low incomes are involuntarily poor.

Finally, it should be noted that more than 6 million immigrants, most of them very poor, arrived in the United States during the decade of the 1970s. (An equal number is entering during the 1980s.) Although most arrive poor, the vast majority does not long remain poor, even by official figures. Most quickly seize the immense opportunities available to them.

b. Income and Wealth: The final draft (no. 182) finds the distribution of income in the United States "unacceptable." But this means that the distributions of income in all but a handful of smaller, more culturally homogeneous nations (such as Sweden, the Netherlands, Denmark), are also "unacceptable." Since hardly a score of nations in all of human history have done better in this respect, the final draft would appear to find most life on earth "unacceptable." Most Americans who have high incomes today arose from poor families, and many descendants of formerly high-income families now experience lesser income. In America, there is a very rapid churning—up and down—among income groups. Income patterns are not stationary. Income does not arrive through political privilege; it must be earned.

In addition, for any one individual, income varies by age. Most persons pass through several different income quintiles during their lifetime. Most attain the apogee of their annual income from ages 40 to 55. Both before and after that period, they tend to be in lower quintiles. Moreover, on the whole, those who invest years of study in higher education (during which, statistically, they appear in the lowest quintile), eventually receive above-average incomes. Measures of inequality must be corrected for age distributions and differences in educational attainment.

The unusually large cohort of the "baby boom," born between 1945 and 1965, began entering the low end of the income statistics in about 1965. Until about 1980, their unusually large presence in the national statistical profile ("like a pig in a python") served to swell the lower income quintiles. More members of the baby boom generation have received university educations than any other generation, so it is no wonder that, as they grow older, their above-average incomes begin to swell the ranks of the upper two quintiles. During the 1980s, more and more Americans have begun receiving incomes in excess of $31,500 per annum (the threshold for the top two quintiles in 1984). Among more than half of them, both spouses are income earners. Thus, the number of American households earning between $31,500 and $73,000 (the threshold for the top five percent) is at an unprecedented level. From 1970 to 1984, the number of households earning $50,000 or more has grown from 6.5 million to over 11 million. Is this unfair or immoral? On the contrary, it is a sign of the system's considerable moral and financial health.

In 1983, the percentage of tax returns reporting more than $100,000 in income (an income about nine times larger than the official poverty level of $11,000) was only 1 percent. This includes movie stars, athletes, pop singers, inventors, authors, television personalities, some lawyers and doctors and farmers, many small businessmen, as well as executives of major corporations, government, universities, and other institutions. Is it "unacceptable" that about 1 percent of households earns more than $100,000 per year"? Particularly, if most of these did not inherit, but earned, such income?

It is difficult to understand the reasoning of the final draft in no. 182. The draft argues that current distributions of income in the United States are unacceptable "as long as there are poor, hungry, and homeless people in our midst." But a mere $45 billion in cash income would raise *all* persons in the United States above the poverty line, independently of the noncash benefits (far in excess of that amount) already funded. This could be done, even if current income distributions remained as they are. Consider the following two proposals. Helping the "poor, hungry, and homeless" could be done without significantly changing income distributions. Income distributions could be changed without helping the "poor, hungry, and homeless." Since the two issues are notionally quite different, the true impulse in no. 182 is not easy to discern. Clearly, it is not practicality. It can hardly be envy, or even guilt, since it is not wrong for bishops to maintain a standard of living suitable to their station, which certainly places them in the 80 to 95 percent range of all incomes (for 1984, between $45,300 and $73,230), if not in the top 5 percent (above $73,230).

c. Taxation: The final draft expresses a preference for "progressive taxation," but without describing the actual results of the pre-1985 tax system in the United States. In 1983 approximately 100 million households and individuals paid income taxes. Twenty percent of all income taxes were paid by the top 1 percent of income earners. Nearly 70 percent were paid by the top 20 percent. Less than 5 percent were paid by the bottom 40 percent. This seems reasonably fair—those with higher incomes paid more taxes. But there is also a curious wrinkle.

The final draft does not advert to the crucial difference between tax *rates* and tax *revenues*. Beginning in 1981, the U.S. Congress lowered tax *rates* for everybody. Yet the effect has been, year by year, that the high-income households—even at lower *rates*—have been paying higher amounts (and proportions) of actual taxes paid. In other words, lower rates bring in more taxes from higher-income persons than higher rates did.

Based upon this experience, beginning in 1986, Congress "flattened" U.S. tax rates considerably, leaving only four "progressive" rates, and lowering existing rates for everyone. The poor and the near-poor no longer pay any income tax at all. Tax exemptions for each child go up. The expected result is that taxes for couples with children earning below $20,000 either disappear or drop substantially. Nonetheless, while almost everyone will be taxed at lower *rates* than before, the government's actual *intake* from taxes will probably go up, and the proportion of all taxes paid by the wealthy should rise significantly.

In short, tax *rates* change incentives, behaviors, and amounts of taxes actually raised by governments. A merely "progressive" scheme of tax rates is not sufficiently sophisticated. One can *lower* tax rates, and even "flatten" them considerably, and still gain more revenue than before from high-income quintiles. To benefit the common good, it is not necessary to be punitive toward earners of high income. One can gain higher actual revenues from them by lowering rates. These are empirical propositions, confirmed by recent experience, but falsifiable by contrary experience.

By contrast, the final draft approaches high-income earners in an adversarial tone. It fails to note the high proportion of taxes paid by the top quintile in 1985. It fails to foresee the probability that, after the tax reform of 1986, the top quintile will probably pay an even higher proportion of all taxes paid.

Far from having led the way to tax reform, the three drafts of the Pastoral Letter have so far been left behind by events.

   d. Welfare: Because most analysts of the experiments in welfare since 1965 have come to see the role of family life as crucial to the poor, many laypersons had expected the Catholic bishops to lay great stress on Catholic teaching regarding the family. While 5 million of the poor live alone, the vast majority of the U.S. poor (about 26 of 33 million in 1985) lives in 7 million poor families. Half of these are the result of separation, divorce, or having children out of wedlock. No other cause of poverty ranks as high as family breakdown. Looked at from another perspective, there are 50.4 million "intact" families in the United States. Of those, only 6.8 percent are poor; 93.2 percent are not. To keep husband and wife together is one of the best routes out of poverty.

   One million poor families in 1985 fell below the poverty line by less than $1,000; another million by less than $2,000; and so on. Since poverty statistics reflect pre-tax income, the 1986 tax law exempting the poor from all income taxes will not change their official status; but it will change their condition, by leaving more money in their hands.

   Despite this nation's many successes in raising up the poor, the question does remain of those less fortunate persons who are unable to participate happily and fruitfully in our economy. Catholics must respond to the moral imperative to "love our neighbor," especially those neighbors who fall into the category of the involuntarily poor. But as we noted in our Lay Letter, *Toward the Future,* it is important to see precisely who the poor are and what their many, diverse needs are. Lumping the poor together in one undifferentiated mass is likely to result in errant, wasteful, and ineffective public policies. For example, not all the poor are trapped in dispiriting cycles. The so-called "underclass" has become highly visible in the media recently, although poor blacks in predominantly poor metropolitan areas constitute only a small fraction (about 16 percent) of the poor.

   The final draft recommends a nationalization of welfare benefits, probably with the expectation that the low-benefit states will thus be brought up to the level of the high-benefit states. Political reality suggests that the opposite is the more likely result. This does not seem to be what the bishops intend.

Welfare policy in the United States is chiefly the responsibility of states. Since economic, cultural, and institutional factors affect the fifty states differently, the principle of subsidiarity would seem to commend the course of federalism rather than the course of nationalization. Some of the differences among states may be almost as extreme as among the nations of continental Europe, and a single continental welfare policy for Europe would no doubt be unworkable. In addition, welfare policy in the United States is probably well served by having the different states try different experiments, so as to learn from each other.

To give the 7 million poor families in the United States $11,000 every year would cost only $77 billion. Current welfare programs disburse larger sums than that. So there is reason to believe that a revolution in our thinking about welfare is urgently needed. Despite vast expenditures of funds, too many sufferings continue, too many pathologies linger, and too many lives fall into dependency and cycles of despair. It has, therefore, become clear to most analysts, left and right, that the problem of welfare is not primarily monetary. Who better than bishops can address the moral dimensions of welfare payments? Welfare programs should be designed to inspire self-reliance, autonomy, fruitful and lasting marriages, and a sense of personal dignity based upon achievement. If human dignity is rooted in work, welfare should also include a component of work for those who can work. There is much to be said about welfare reform that cannot be said professionally by social scientists but that bishops could say. The moral dimension of welfare is crucial.

Analysts are no longer ignoring the moral factor; namely, the role of character, moral obligation, and the public ethos. A demand for benefits without a correlative acceptance of social duties, permissive sexual standards, pregnancies apart from marriage, separation and divorce, and a general shift from self-control to "self-expression" have injured the economic chances of several million of our fellow citizens. Consider the burdens of female-headed households. If the percentage of Americans living in such households had remained at 1959 levels (8 percent), there would have been 7 million fewer poor persons in 1984, all other factors held constant.

One of the most effective social-justice programs today is the private parochial school operating in our nation's inner cities. These schools offer a stable, moral environment in which poor children learn a special respect for hard work, charity, intellectual accomplishment, and self-discipline. We can think of few institutions more worthy of our support than the inner-city private and parochial schools, many hard-pressed by financial difficulties.

Again, the problem of poverty requires more than a monetary response, however necessary that may be. A reinvigoration of our Jewish and Christian moral traditions would open up a crucial second front in the war on poverty. Ironically, the bishop's Pastoral Letter still lacks a clear call for attention to the spiritual and psychological dimensions of poverty.

e. Unemployment: Contrary to the suggestion that our economy has been weak in providing job opportunities, over 30 million jobs have been created in the United States in the fifteen years since 1972, more than 10 million in the four years 1983–1987. Moreover, in speaking of unemployment the final draft fails to note the incredible ease with which, each year, about 9 percent of all Americans voluntarily quit their jobs. This personal choice usually involves some weeks "between jobs." This social fact, uncommon elsewhere in the world, helps to explain why more than half of all the U.S. unemployed are out of work *for at most fifteen weeks.* The sufferings of those, particularly older men or women with families, who are involuntarily out of work for longer periods is keen. It depreciates that suffering to lump such persons without distinction among those who prefer to pick and choose among available jobs, until the right one (in income and in conditions of employment) comes along. There is a profound moral difference between workers with a "preference schedule" and those willing to do whatever is required, but unable to find it. Among the latter, there is real suffering to be addressed.

Again, powerful evidence demonstrates that the "work ethic" is stronger than ever in the United States, at least as measured by the proportion of adults actually employed. A record-setting percentage of civilian Americans over the age of sixteen are employed (61 percent, as of July 1986, compared to 56 percent in 1975). In past years of low unemployment (e.g., 4.5 percent in 1965) a significantly lower proportion of adults was actually employed (56 percent). In some ways the percentage of the employed is a more telling indicator than the percentage of the unemployed. The latter cannot be fully understood without the former. It should, nevertheless, be noted that since the bishops completed their letter, the unemployment rate has declined significantly—another sign of a strong economy.

Finally, the final draft fails to anticipate the severe labor shortage certain to appear in the 1990s as the much smaller cohort behind the "baby boom" comes of age. Declining birth rates already worry employers. In order to attract workers, service establishments are now offering up to twice the minimum wage ($14,000 per year). At places the final draft disparages "low-paying, high-turnover jobs," while failing to recognize how such jobs meet the temporary needs of many employees.

9. The Hunger for Moral Guidance

The American people have been blessed from the beginning with a tradition of sound moral habits. In the press, ordinary virtues are not news; such simple habits as honesty, candor, initiative, inventiveness, practicality, teamwork, and courtesy are common among our population and have important social consequences. A lie told in public has the power to shock; in private, it may mark the end of a friendship. Sloth and irresponsibility in co-workers are not appreciated. Moreover, Americans place unusual emphasis upon the practice of social virtues beyond the family. Americans join many associations and go to many meetings. They tend to be extroverted and associative, rather than introverted and loners.

In such ways, Americans exhibit the virtues proper to the institutions of democratic, capitalist, and pluralistic societies. The virtues proper to American society are not the same as those proper to traditionalist societies. Every social system both depends upon and encourages certain habits, inhibiting others. As Americans grow more prosperous and judge their own conditions by higher and higher standards, some—it is true—price themselves out of some labor markets and regard certain forms of employment as unattractive. As in the past, newer immigrants find precisely the same opportunities quite liberating, compared to what they have known before. In this way, classic American virtues renew their relevance.

In *The Cultural Contradictions of Capitalism,* Daniel Bell argues that the economic success of capitalism changes the ideas and morals of the populations, and that the breaking point in our three systems lies primarily in the moral and cultural system. But the moral and cultural system is precisely the system most entrusted to the care of moral and cultural leaders—such as professors, filmmakers, television personalities, the press, teachers, the clergy, and the bishops. When the moral-cultural system becomes relativist or "permissive," the habits necessary for self-government in politics and for concern about the future in the economic system are undermined. For this reason, many Americans long for greater moral guidance from moral leaders. Betrayal by moral and cultural leaders tears the social fabric. A "breakdown of morals" makes both democracy and capitalism unworkable. When a sense of personal responsibility falters, such necessary virtues as impulse-restraint, self-mastery, self-reliance, and mutual cooperation falter. Without these, institutions based upon self-government and personal responsibility cannot function. In our judgment, the American people cry out for moral leadership; but too many moral and cultural leaders are silent about a relatively permissive personal morality, and prefer to declaim on politics.

10. "Economic Justice for All" Must Be Preceded by Economic Justice for Nuns

The credibility of a Pastoral Letter on *Economic Justice for All* will be undermined if all of us together in the Catholic church—laypersons, clergy, and bishops—do not immediately remove the scandal of the economic poverty of nuns abandoned in their old age, without pensions, obliged to turn to the state rather than to the church for assistance. During so many years, these valiant women have given us so much, in schools, in hospitals, and in untold works of mercy. Each of us recalls individuals among them with great gratitude. For us, they have been the salt of the earth. In their old age, they deserve the best from us. The stories we now hear of them, dependent in their old age upon food stamps and welfare, shame our consciences. Our Lay Commission is eager to help raise a pension fund that would support them in independent dignity. This is a high priority of justice and love.

Summary

For all these reasons, we are grateful to our bishops for opening up a dialogue—in time for the two-hundredth anniversary of the U.S. Constitution—on moral and foundational issues. We also thank them for the open manner in which they have proceeded, and for inviting public criticism and debate. In response, we have tried to meet our own responsibilities as lay Catholics. What the final draft has done well, we admire. We welcome *especially* its emphasis upon lifting up the poor.

On the other hand, we believe that in several of its empirical descriptions, in some of its political and economic conceptions, and in many of its practical recommendations, the bishops' letter falls short of its own manifest intentions. It intends to help the poor. In several key respects, it is likely to hurt those it intends to help. We are especially sad that it falls short of a full understanding of the American experiment in economics, fully original and fully as exemplary as its experiment in political and civil liberties.

Note

1. Quoted in George F. Will, "The Illusion of Arms Control," *Newsweek,* 13 October 1986, 102.

2

Virtue in Catholic Social Teaching

J. Brian Benestad

Love of God and neighbor is the supreme principle of Christian social morality.[1] From this commandment, St. Augustine writes, "arise the duties pertaining to human society about which it is difficult not to err."[2] This simple thought sounds foreign and even cynical to many today. For they know the shape of the just social order and are certain that it can be achieved—if only the proper structures are created.

Modern Catholic social teaching echoes the Augustinian realism regarding the imperfection of the world and the intractability of its problems. Like Augustine's message, it does not lose heart in the face of difficulties. Instead it assumes the task of providing guidance so that people may err a little less in their duties toward society. While avoiding utopianism, Catholic social teaching still makes bold statements, especially regarding virtue. It helps people learn and live what it means to love God and neighbor in practice. In other words, it attempts to determine what are the political and social conditions favorable to Christian life. It also tries to explain which sets of institutions and practices best express justice toward God and neighbor, which foster genuine community among men and women, and which character traits and institutional arrangements promote the common good.[3]

The doctrine of the church does not advocate any particular social, economic, or political system. It does, however, offer principles for reflection, criteria for judgment, and directives for action—all of which serve as standards for judging whether particular systems fulfill the requirements of human dignity.[4] Catholic social teaching is not based solely on revelation and tradition, but also on the resources of human wisdom and the sciences. Consequently, this teaching contains both permanently valid principles and contingent judgments.[5] In other words, Catholic social teaching can change in a way that Catholic teaching on faith and morals cannot.

Catholic social teaching is a supplement to, rather than a replacement of, the indirect impact on society of the church's traditional ministries. Its very existence shows that the church takes seriously the obligation that Christians be the "salt of the earth" and the "light of the world." It shows also that the church responds to the prayer made to the Lord, "Give us this day our daily bread."

The most important contribution of Catholic social doctrine to the American mind is its teaching on virtue. In the words of Cardinal Ratzinger, prefect of the Sacred Congregation for the Doctrine of the Faith, "the first thing to be done is to appeal to the spiritual and moral capacities of the individual and to the permanent need for inner conversion, if one is to achieve the economic and social changes that will truly be at the service of man."[6] The *first thing* is not to look to the market, or the government, or even some combination thereof in order to achieve social justice, but to virtue. Unless many individuals practice virtue the modern state cannot secure the public interest. In order to understand and practice virtue, however, people need healthy families, religious training, and sound education. Hence the relevance of these themes in Catholic social teaching.

Subsidiarity

Taking a look at the principle of subsidiarity is a good way to begin the study of Catholic social teaching. Pope Pius XI's social encyclical *Quadragesimo Anno,* published in 1931, contains the classic twentieth-century statement of that principle. More recently, the National Conference of Catholic Bishops (NCCB) reintroduced subsidiarity to Americans by including some of Pius XI's remarks in their own *Economic Justice for All: Pastoral Letter on Catholic Social Teaching and the U.S. Economy,* issued in 1986.

Just as it is gravely wrong to take from individuals what they can accomplish by their own initiative and industry and give it to the community, so also it is an injustice and at the same time a grave evil and disturbance of right order to assign to a greater and higher association what lesser and subordinate organizations can do. For every social activity ought of its very nature to furnish help *(subsidium)* to the members of the body social, and never destroy and absorb them.[7]

The remainder of Pius XI's reflections on subsidiarity is not quoted in the U.S. bishops' letter but reads as follows:

The supreme authority of the state ought, therefore, to let subordinate groups handle matters and concerns of lesser importance, which would otherwise dissipate its efforts greatly. Thereby the state will more freely, powerfully, and effectively do all those things that belong to it alone because it alone can do them: directing, watching, urging, restraining, as occasion requires and necessity demands. Therefore, those in power should be sure that the more perfectly a graduated order is kept among the various associations, in observance of the principle of "subsidiary function," the stronger social authority and effectiveness will be and the happier and more prosperous the conditions of the state.[8]

The NCCB Pastoral Letter points out that the principle of subsidiarity establishes need for vital contributions from different human associations ranging in size from the family to the government.[9] The preservation of this principle gives individuals, mediating structures, and government (local, state, and national) an opportunity to make a contribution to the common good. When subsidiarity prevails, the government does not take over the functions of private associations, and the latter do not usurp the initiative and responsibility of individuals. On the other hand, subsidiarity requires state intervention when associations and individuals are not able to fulfill the requirements of the common good. Disagreements, of course, are inevitable in determining the most beneficial mix of government intervention and private initiative, and that determination depends on political prudence. It is at least clear, however, that subsidiarity requires rejection of extremist theories of government such as pure communism or radical individualism.

Not surprisingly, the bishops' letter on the economy generated disagreement over the application of the principle of subsidiarity.

Critics of the letter claimed that the bishops advocate too much state intervention. The bishops and their supporters respond that conservative critics rely too much on the market to promote the common good. Both sides disagree on which government policies are most beneficial to economic well-being. The debate over the proper mix of government intervention and private initiative, as well as the wisdom of this or that policy, is, of course, important, but not the heart of the matter. Too much emphasis on structural change in the form of policy or reliance on the market—as the key to the common good—obscures the countercultural aspects of Catholic social teaching, especially reflections on virtue, the family, education, and the common good.

Structures vs. Virtue

Despite the recent publication of pastoral letters on war and peace and the U.S. economy, Catholic social teaching remains relatively unknown to Catholics, not to mention the wider public. Both pastoral letters contain summaries of Catholic social teaching, including statements of moral principle, but they are incomplete. More important, the main focus of the letters is on political change in the form of particular policy improvements. Not surprisingly the media pays little attention to the bishops' statements regarding moral principles.

The Pastoral Letter on the economy provides a striking example of the importance placed by the bishops themselves on "declarations of principle." In the important Pastoral Message affixed to the letter on the economy, they say, "The Church's teachings cannot be left at the level of 'appealing generalities' " when there is the obligation and the opportunity to "teach by example how Christians can undertake concrete analysis and make specific judgments on economic issues."[10] Establishing and modifying structures, in this view, seems to be much more effective than attempting to establish a public morality or educating people to virtue.

As to the wisdom of stressing structures or virtue, the Sacred Congregation for the Doctrine of the Faith (SCDF) provides guidance. In its *Instruction on Christian Freedom and Liberation* issued March 22, 1986, the author of the document, Cardinal Ratzinger, explains: "The priority given to structures and technical organization over the person and the requirements of his dignity is the expression of a materialistic anthropology and is contrary to the construction of a just social order."[11]

The central affirmation of Catholic social teaching is the permanent need for conversion, without which the attempt to establish a just social order or the common good of society is in vain. This is not a new theme but has been a part of Catholic political wisdom all the way back to the church fathers. St. Augustine highlighted the importance of virtue for social life in his influential *City of God:* "When a man does not serve God, what justice can we ascribe to him, since in this case his soul cannot exercise a just control over the body, nor his reason over his vices. And if there is no justice in such an individual, certainly there can be none in a community of such persons."[12]

From the 1960s on, the understanding of a just social order grounded in virtue has been obscured in the minds of many, including bishops, priests, and theologians. In a recent interview on the state of the church, Cardinal Ratzinger felt obliged to say:

> It is also painful to be confronted with the illusion, so essentially un-Christian, which is present among priests and theologians that a new man and a new world can be created not by calling each individual to conversion, but only by changing the social and economic structures. Those who desire a more human society need to begin with the root not with the trunk and branches of the tree of injustice. The issue here is one of fundamental Christian truths, yet they are depreciatingly dismissed as alienating and "spiritualistic."[13]

This stress on structures is really an attempt to circumvent human imperfection. Catholic political wisdom used to hold that society cannot be good unless individuals are good. In other words, individual moral efforts remain indispensable under every form of government. The new approach hopes to overcome the limits of relying on conversion and virtue. The change from sinful to just structures will effect a moral change in society and in individuals. In this new perspective, says Ratzinger, "It is not ethics that supports structures, but structures support ethics for the reason namely that ethics is fragile while structures are regarded as solid and sure."[14]

Excessive reliance on structures for social benefits is also evident in the original philosophical theory supporting capitalism. One essential component of that theory held that private vices by an invisible hand would produce public benefits. In other words, the pursuit of one's own interest, however selfish, would necessarily benefit other individuals. Ratzinger explains, "The market's inner logic should free us precisely from the necessity of having to depend on the morality of its participants."[15] Morality becomes dispensable, according to the theory, because the operation of the market is deterministic. "It presupposes that the free play of the market can operate in *one* direction only, given the constitution of man and the world, namely toward the self-regulation of supply and demand, and toward economic efficiency and progress."[16]

The centralized economy of Marxism would seem to have nothing in common with the free market of liberal capitalism. Yet there is a Marxist equivalent of the liberal belief that public good inevitably results from the individual pursuit of self-interest. Marxists believe that history inevitably guarantees the attainment of the public good through class struggle and the collectivization of property. Marxism, in fact, is inseparable from a dialectic of history and, thus, from a deterministic view of things and, as such, also dispenses with the need for wisdom and virtue.

The ironic aspect of this debate over structures is not without educational value. Neither the bishops nor most of their critics would recognize in themselves any lack of appreciation for the role of conversion and virtue in promoting a just social order. Ratzinger's criticism of those giving priority to structural change over conversion and virtue would seem, then, to apply to no identifiable individuals or groups. Either Ratzinger's comments are off the mark or the American Catholic way of understanding and discussing virtue is incomplete.

Approaches to Virtue

In order to understand the relevance of Ratzinger's criticisms, it is helpful to reflect on the problem and meaning of virtue. Virtue is not a major theme of Catholic moral theology today, nor apparently of Catholic catechetical programs, in the United States. The typical college student at a Catholic university can hardly name a virtue, much less distinguish the cardinal from the theological virtues. If there is ignorance about virtue itself, the connection between virtue and the common good is even more unfamiliar to many Americans. In thinking about the public interest, most educated Americans, including Catholics, would surely rely mainly on concepts like human rights, social justice, liberty, equality, compassion, fairness, values, and the dignity of the human person.

Cardinal Ratzinger's reflections on freedom and sin in his *Instruction on Christian Freedom and Liberation* provide a good introduction to the Catholic concept of virtue. Christian freedom, he explains, is primarily freedom from sin and death brought about by the death and resurrection of Jesus Christ. Since sin and death are the greatest evils, greater than poverty and oppression even, the redemption wrought by Jesus Christ is the most radical liberation.

Sin is contempt for God and disordered love of self. Sin is the practical rejection of the truth about human existence. By sinning, people lie to themselves and deny the reality that stares them in the face. Through sin "man rejects the truth and places his own will above it." Sin is self-destructive because the sinner does not harmonize "his will with his nature," and the disorder in the sinner's heart inevitably causes disorder in the family, in government, and in all of society.[17]

Christianity frees people to act according to their natures and, therefore, to be good. Ratzinger says further: "The good is the goal of freedom. In consequence, man becomes free to the extent that he comes to a knowledge of the truth—and to the extent that this truth—and not any other forces—guides his will."[18] Christian liberation, then, depends on maintaining the link among truth, goodness, and freedom. There can be no freedom unless the human person can come to a knowledge of the good.

Thomas Aquinas says that virtue "makes a man good, and renders his work good."[19] People achieve goodness by acting according to reason and divine law. While virtue enables a person to act in accord with reason and divine law, sin creates obstacles to doing so. In other words, inordinate love of pleasure, money, power, honor, and glory, as well as anger, resentment, sloth, anxiety, ignorance, and the like, lead people away from the good. It is not hard to see how these disordered passions in turn have negative, sometimes devastating, consequences for families, large social units, and governments.

There are other approaches to understanding virtue, one of which is through the concept, familiar within Catholic social teaching, of the dignity of the human person. Vatican Council II says that "the root reason for human dignity lies in man's call to communion with God."[20] Made in God's image, human beings are capable of knowing and loving their Creator. This said, the next comment is usually about rights. Because human beings have dignity, they must be protected by rights—political, civil, and socioeconomic—and the protection of rights requires adequate structures. Thus the dignity of the human person, the foundation stone of Catholic social thought, requires attention first and foremost to structures, especially public policy. So the argument runs, but it runs too quickly, missing some important points. Vatican II's Declaration on Religious Liberty says that people attain true dignity when they seek truth and live their lives in accord with truth.[21] In the measure that people sin and fail to love God and neighbor, they fail to achieve the dignity God intended. The dignity of the human person thus depends primarily on the practice of virtue, especially charity, but also on prudence, justice, temperance, and fortitude. St. Augustine called these four virtues "the fourfold disposition of love itself."[22]

Intimately linked to the dignity of the human person is the principle of solidarity. According to this principle, all people have an obligation "to contribute to the common good of society at all its levels."[23] Accordingly, church doctrine opposes any form of political or social individualism. In other words, people realize their dignity by exercising duties toward the commonwealth and society—for example, by being good citizens, by doing their work well, and by setting high standards within their trades and professions.

If human dignity requires avoiding sin and practicing virtue, the argument that leaps from dignity over virtue to rights is unconvincing. Besides, while rights are important for achieving the protection of life, liberty, and property, they are not self-enforcing. In the absence of virtue, self-interest or fear is needed to guarantee them. For example, what is to keep people from disregarding the rights of others if they can do so and still have their own rights respected?

While Catholic social teaching does of course defend rights, it always links rights to duties and divine law. *Pacem in Terris,* Pope John XXIII's social encyclical, says that the chief duty of every public authority is to "safeguard the inviolable rights of the human person in order to facilitate the fulfillment of his duties."[24] Vatican II's *Guadium et Spes* adds that human dignity is annihilated if rights are proclaimed apart from the divine law.[25]

Not even such a brief treatment of virtue as this could be considered adequate without a look at the virtue of prudence. Prudence, says Thomas Aquinas, is right reason applied to action, which cannot be done unless the passions are appropriately moderated. Reason, for Thomas Aquinas, means openness to reality. With respect to knowing reality, Joseph Pieper, a well-known Thomist scholar, comments:

> The pre-eminence of prudence means that realization of the good presupposes knowledge of reality. He alone can do good who knows what things are like and what their situation is. The pre-eminence of prudence means that so-called "good intentions" and so-called "meaning well" by no means suffice.[26]

In order to make a prudent decision, people need knowledge of principles and singulars. Without principles, they have a hard time not accepting prevailing trends as normative. Without a knowledge of singulars, the application of principles is at least ineffective, if not harmful.

Thomas Aquinas believes that everyone in the state of grace is virtuous and, therefore, prudent. Prudence, however, can be corrupted by the passions. Thomas explains:

> For the philosopher [Aristotle] says (Ethics, VI, 5) that pleasure and sorrow pervert the estimate of prudence: wherefore it is written (Dan. 13:56):—"Beauty hath deceived thee, and lust hath subverted thy heart," and (Exod. 33:8): "Neither shalt thou take bribes which blind even the prudent."[27]

An unchaste man, for example, cannot see objective reality. Pieper comments:

> His constantly strained will to pleasure prevents him from confronting reality with that selfless detachment which alone makes genuine knowledge possible. St. Thomas here uses the comparison of a lion who, at the sight of a stag, is unable to perceive anything but the anticipated meal.[28]

Still another example is the effect of resentment and anger on perception. For example, many Catholic intellectuals today feel such anger against Rome that they are closed to taking seriously some points of view merely because they originate or emanate from the Vatican.

While every virtuous person is prudent, not all are equally so with respect to all things. Every virtuous person can be diligent with respect to things necessary for one's salvation, but not all can deliberate equally well about the common good. Thomas explains:

> There is also another diligence which is more than sufficient whereby a man is able to make provision both for himself and for others, not only in matters necessary for salvation, but also in all things relating to human life; and such diligence as this is not in all who have grace.[29]

Prudence, then, deals not only with the private good of the individual, but also with the common good of all. St. Thomas says that "the prudence that is directed to the common good is called political prudence."[30] That enough people have this prudence is crucial for the well-being of all individuals. Thomas goes so far as to say that "the individual good is impossible without the common good of the family, state or kingdom."[31] For example, children from families where there is little or no education to virtue have great difficulty understanding what is good and noble.

Political prudence depends on native abilities, education, and experience. Familiarity with history, politics, economics, political philosophy, and other things are very important for seeing the big picture. For example, it would be difficult if not impossible to understand the strengths and weaknesses of liberal democracy—as well as possible remedies for those weaknesses—without a working knowledge of politics and political philosophy.

Liberal education is hard to acquire these days, even in Catholic universities. Besides, the typical college student has very little interest in matters pertaining to the common good. Reflecting on liberal education today, Allan Bloom observes that almost every college freshman believes, or says he or she believes, that truth is relative.[32] The pervasiveness of ethical relativism, Bloom explains, "has extinguished the real motive of education, the search for a good life."[33] If truth varies from age to age or from person to

person, then there is no reason to get excited about reading Jane
Austen, the Bible, or Plato. As a matter of fact, many students have
lost their taste for reading altogether.

Not reading good books makes students prisoners of the here
and now and deprives them of any "resource whatsoever against
conformity to the current 'role models.' " Without books young
people cannot conceive of what human excellence might be. "Deprived of literary guidance, they no longer have any image of a
perfect soul, and hence do not long to have one." Bloom rightly
places stress on the absence of ideas and longings in the modern
student, whose passivity almost defies belief.

Besides the intellectual slackness, Bloom also notes a strong
stream of self-centeredness in today's students. They "are, in
general, nice," but "not particularly moral or noble." "Neither
duty nor pleasure involves students with the political. The petty
personal interests of youth—'making it,' finding a place for oneself—perseveres through life." Students feel no particular inclina-
tion to be citizens. They really accept the philosophic and economic
principle that private vice by an invisible hand produces public
benefits.[34]

Bloom points out that, shortly after Hitler came to power in 1933,
the famous German philosopher Martin Heidegger addressed the
university community in Freiburg. He "urged commitment to National Socialism" and "put philosophy (and the university) at the
service of the reigning German culture." Bloom believes that what
happened to the German universities in the 1930s "is what has
happened and is happening everywhere."[35] The American university ministers to the needs of society, not vice versa. In other
words, the university has lost its identity (and its objectivity) by
simply serving contemporary culture. It no longer offers a correc-
tive to the kinds of problems endemic to American liberal democracy, such as subservience to public opinion, concentration on the
useful, distaste for the theoretical life, acceptance of deterministic
explanations of events, and proneness to abstractions such as
Freudianism and economism.

Bloom insists that the main task of the university is to keep alive
the permanent questions that everyone faces—God, love, death,
truth, justice, the common good, and so forth. An intelligent
reading of the great books, Bloom believes, is the best way to

accomplish this task. Studying the great books with care ensures real openness, not the kind that puts the face of high principle on accommodation to powerful trends in society or the academy. "True openness means closedness to all the charms that make us comfortable with the present."[36]

A good liberal education revives the low aspirations of students; it can refine their inchoate longings for clarity about the meaning of the good life and the meaning of justice. Liberal education, properly understood, does not teach values—as many are urging these days—but gives *reasons;* and good reasons, tempered by charity and justice, are the soul of political prudence.

Economic Justice for All

While the American bishops' Pastoral Letter on the economy stresses primarily prudential policy judgments, it does contain a chapter on ethical principles. A brief look at selected points in this chapter helps to illustrate some themes and problems of Catholic social teaching.

The biblical section affirms that God fashioned man and woman in his image and tells the story of the eruption of sin into the world. Summarizing the biblical teaching on sin, the letter says: "Sin simultaneously alienates human beings from God and then shatters the solidarity of the human community."[37] The only example of sin given in this section is the misuse of the world's resources, that is, the appropriation of them by a minority of the world's population.[38] The Pastoral Letter passes up the opportunity to explain in any detail the meaning of sin and the many ways in which sin disrupts the social and political order. This is disturbing in the light of the fact that many Catholics, especially the young, are experiencing great difficulty understanding the very concept of sin. How sin affects social and political life approaches the category of mystery for many.

The second major theme under the heading of biblical perspectives is that of the covenant. The letter explains how God's initiative in entering into a covenant with the Israelites provides a solid foundation for ethics. "The quest for justice arises from loving gratitude for the saving acts of God and manifests itself in wholehearted love of God and neighbor."[39] This very important point needs some elaboration. Being just and loving God are really acts of gratitude for God's many deeds, which people know through faith. In other words, virtue as gratitude depends on a firm belief that, in fact, God has demonstrated his love for human beings through creation, the exodus, and so forth.

The section entitled "Ethical Norms for Economic Life" begins with a discussion of people's duties toward one another and the whole community, under the rubric of love, justice, and the special obligation toward the poor and vulnerable. By speaking of duties before rights, the bishops make a significant countercultural statement: In a society dominated by the language of rights, talk of duties brings a new dimension to the discussion of public morality in the United States.[40] The bishops, however, blunt their praiseworthy initiative, first, by affixing a Pastoral Message to their letter containing six moral principles that focus entirely on rights and, second, by emphasizing structural reform, rather than virtue, in the section on duties.

In their Pastoral Message, the bishops list six principles taken from Scripture and the social teaching of the church. While not complete as a summary of all the principles in the letter, they do give an overview of the bishops' moral vision. According to these principles, the good life is one in which society, acting through government and voluntary associations, protects human dignity by surrounding people with civil rights, political rights, and economic rights—as well as by organizing society in economics and politics, in law and policy. The only obligation mentioned among the six principles is that of every citizen toward the poor and vulnerable. There is also a passing reference to the policy dimension of the obligation to "love our neighbor."[41] Unfortunately, the bishops do not do justice to themselves in their list of six principles. Their moral vision is actually deeper than these principles would lead people to believe.

The section on duties begins well. Love of God and love of neighbor "are the heart and soul of Christian morality."[42] Through these two kinds of love, Christians foster communion among themselves and with God. Through the virtues of citizenship, which are an expression of love, people build up the civic community by promoting solidarity among various groups in society. The letter mentions two serious obstacles to the fulfillment of duties toward the commonweal—ignorance and sin—but offers no explanation of them. The means of seeking, and the difficulty of attaining, political prudence might have been discussed here.

The Pastoral Letter's emphasis on structural change at the expense of virtue is very apparent in the section on justice. "Social justice implies that persons have an obligation to be active and productive participants in the life of society and that society has a duty to enable them to participate in this way."[43] There are two parts to this description of social justice. First, individuals have a duty to promote the common good by contributing goods and services to society. As an explanation of this statement the letter cites a sentence from Pius XI: "It is of the very essence of social justice to demand from each individual all that is necessary for the common good."[44] An examination of *Quadragesimo Anno* reveals that Pope Pius XI stresses the correction of morals, or a return to virtue, as the principal means of realizing social justice and the common good. Virtue is, thus, clearly an essential means to restoring society, but it is also an end in itself. Virtue is never something simply personal or private.

The second aspect of social justice is the reform of institutions, upon which the Pastoral Letter lays more stress than on a correction of morals in view of the common good. As examples of structural reforms, the letter mentions the following: assurance of adequate employment, overcoming of discrimination through affirmative-action programs, establishment of a floor of material well-being for all, reduction of extreme inequalities in income and consumption, and a system of taxation based on the ability to pay. To overcome extreme inequality, the bishops assert that Americans "must resist the temptation constantly to seek more."

The section on social justice concludes with this remarkable statement: "The concentration of privilege that exists today results far more from institutional relationships that distribute power and wealth inequitably than from differences in talent or lack of desire to work."[45] This remark goes a long way toward explaining episcopal emphasis on social justice as structural reform. It implies that institutional relationships, as opposed to talent, hard work, personal desire, education, and family stability, are decisive in causing inequitable distribution of material goods. Work for justice, then, consists mainly in coming up with the kind of public policy that reduces inequality or redistributes income.

The bishops are, of course, correct to point out that social justice requires structural reform, but they are off the mark in not highlighting the connection between virtue and the common good. Emphasizing that connection would have been an important contribution to public morality in the United States.

A summary of the fundamental duties of citizens includes the following remark: "Basic justice demands the establishment of minimum levels of participation in the life of the human community for all persons."[46] Obstacles to participation are restrictions on free speech, state repression, and economic forces that generate poverty. "Justice demands that social institutions be ordered in a way that guarantees all persons the ability to participate actively in the economic, political and cultural life of society."[47] Even political participation depends on social justice in the form of structural reform according to the letter. Other important conditions for citizen participation are omitted: for example, the fact that, because of everyday hardships of life, many people lose heart and barely manage to keep body and soul together, much less contribute to the common good. The bishops surely know that sound education, good family life, and virtues such as fortitude are as important to political participation as employment programs.

The section on duties is brief, and much shorter than the section on human rights. It does indicate that Catholic teaching requires individuals to love one another and to heed the requirements of social justice by contributing to the common good. The emphasis, however, is on the duties of citizens to work for the reform of institutions through public-policy initiatives. The letter sees social reform as that which enables citizens to participate in the life of society, and the greatest benefit of participation as the attainment of an adequate standard of living. In other words, even in the section on duties, the letter lays more stress on receiving benefits than on conferring them, on demanding justice than on being just.

Before concluding this assessment of the Pastoral Letter on the economy, a word about the section of moral priorities. The bishops' moral priorities for the nation focus on increasing the material well-being of the poor and marginalized. While this is obviously a desirable goal, it raises the question whether or not the common good demands other priorities as well, and whether or not the bishops keep the problem of poverty in the proper perspective.

The spirit with which the Pastoral Letter addresses moral priorities is best revealed in its treatment of divorce and poverty. The letter says: "To face family problems, such as the death of a spouse or a divorce, can be devastating, but to have these lead to the loss of one's home and end with living on the streets is something no one should have to endure in a country as rich as ours."[48] While poverty and homelessness are indeed devastating, the bishops might have given more credence to the disastrous pain, both physical and mental, caused by divorce and widespread family breakdown. They might even have committed themselves to the improvement of their own institutions by calling upon all the faithful to reflect, and act where possible, on the problem of family break-up. The church can surely be more industrious and imaginative in helping people to prepare for marriage, to marry well, and to stay together. Professor Allan Bloom's point about the family could not be more true:

> The implicit lesson that the family taught was the existence of the only unbreakable bond, for better or for worse, between human beings. The decomposition of this bond is surely America's most urgent social problem. But nobody ever tries to do anything about it. The tide seems to be irresistible. Among the many items on the agenda of those promoting America's moral regeneration, I never find marriage and divorce.[49]

Conclusion

The contribution of Catholic social doctrine to the American mind in the form of a teaching on virtue has yet to be realized. In order to understand virtue, Catholics need a good knowledge of their faith. By most accounts, that knowledge is lacking these days. The Extraordinary Synod of 1985 stated the problem well.

> Everywhere on earth today the transmission to the young of the faith and moral values deriving from the Gospel is in danger. Often knowledge of the faith and the acceptance of the moral order are reduced to a minimum. Therefore, a new effort in evangelization and in integral and systematic catechesis is required.[50]

Without this effort, it is unlikely that either Catholic social teaching or the political benefits of virtue will be understood. The Catholic church in the United States needs a seamless garment of Catholic teaching in faith and morals, not one limited to a wide range of prudential policy judgments.

Policy involvement is time-consuming and may distract bishops from their main tasks. More important than current policy proposals are such problems as disaffection from the church, ignorance of the faith, the state of seminaries (e.g., the decline of serious interest in philosophy and theology), dissent from the magisterium of the church, the breakdown of the family, the rejection of Catholic moral teaching, and inadequate catechesis. There is now even serious disagreement in the church as to who can authoritatively determine the very meaning of Christianity. Revelation, tradition, and the teaching authority of the church are now competing with the experience, or praxis, of Christian communities and the consensus of contemporary theologians and other intellectuals.

Some supporters of the bishops have welcomed the nonbinding mode of teaching under the category of prophecy. They call for conversion to the bishops' progressive political opinions and then adopt an attitude of intolerance toward any deviance from the "liberal orthodoxy." At the same time, they call for open-mindedness on a variety of opinions about traditional moral questions such as homosexual acts, premarital sex, abortion, artificial contraception, euthanasia, and so on. The result is authoritarianism in the political realm and democratic pluralism in moral theology.

Toward the end of the sixth century, Gregory the Great wrote the *Regula Pastoralis,* a book on the nature and difficulties of the episcopal office. It soon had a great influence on priests and bishops and even on the laity. At one time, it was presented to bishops at the time of their consecration. Gregory reminded pastors not to be so preoccupied with spiritual matters that they neglected the bodily needs of their flock. However, he also pointed out the greater danger: that bishops might neglect their spiritual duties and "devote themselves with all concentration of heart to secular cares."[51] Gregory cites approvingly Jethro's reproach of Moses for spending an inordinate amount of time settling differences among the people. "Hence, Moses, who speaks with God, is judged by the reproof of

Jethro, a man of alien race, on the ground that he devotes himself by his ill-advised labor to the earthly affairs of his people." Moses' father-in-law, Jethro, continues Gregory, does not recommend neglect of those matters, but counsels Moses to delegate the task to others, so that "he may be more free to learn the secrets of spiritual matters for teaching the people."[52] The book of Exodus says that Moses followed the advice of his father-in-law.

Notes

1. Sacred Congregation for the Doctrine of the Faith (SCDF), *Instruction on Christian Freedom and Liberation* (Boston: St. Paul Editions, 1986), no. 71, p. 46.
2. St. Augustine, *The Catholic and Manichean Ways of Life* (Washington, D.C.: The Catholic University of America Press, 1966), p. 40.
3. See Yves de Montcheuil, S. J., *Problemes de vie spirituelle* (Paris: Éditions de L'Epi, 1961), pp. 196–220.
4. SCDF, *Instruction on Christian Freedom and Liberation*, no. 74, pp. 48–49.
5. Ibid., no. 72, p. 47.
6. Ibid., no. 75, p. 49.
7. National Conference of Catholic Bishops (NCCB), *Economic Justice for All: Catholic Social Teaching and the U.S. Economy* (Washington, D.C.: USCC, 1986), p. 51.
8. Pius XI, *Quadragesimo Anno*, no. 80.
9. NCCB, *Economic Justice for All*, pp. 50–51.
10. Ibid., p. xii.
11. SCDF, *Instruction on Christian Freedom and Liberation*, no. 75, p. 49.
12. St. Augustine, *The City of God* (New York: Modern Library, 1950), p. 700.
13. Joseph Cardinal Ratzinger, with Vittorio Messori, *The Ratzinger Report: An Exclusive Interview on the State of the Church* (San Francisco: Ignatius Press, 1985), p. 190.
14. Joseph Cardinal Ratzinger, "Christliche Orientierung in der pluralistichen Demokratie? Uber die Unverzichtbarkeit des Christentums in der modernen Gesellschaft," in *Das Europaische Erbe und Seine Christliche Zukunft,* ed. Nikolaus Lobkowicz (Cologne, West Germany: Hans Martin Schleyer-Stiftung, 1985), p. 23 (trans. J.B.B.).
15. Joseph Cardinal Ratzinger, "Church and Economy: Responsibility for the Future of the World Economy," *Communio* 13, no. 3 (1986): 200.
16. Ibid.
17. SCDF, *Instruction on Christian Freedom and Liberation*, no. 37, pp. 21–22.

18. Ibid., no. 26, p. 16.
19. St. Thomas Aquinas, *Summa Theologica*, II. Q123, Al Benzenger Brothers edition.
20. *The Documents of Vatican Council II*, Walter M. Abbot, S. J., gen. ed. (NY: Herder & Herder, 1966).
21. Ibid.
22. St. Augustine, *The Catholic and Manichean Ways of Life*, no. 25, trans. Donald A. Gallagher and Idella Gallagher (Washington, D.C.: Catholic University of America Press), 22.
23. SCDF, *Instruction on Christian Freedom and Liberation*, no. 73, p. 47.
24. Pope John XXIII, *Pacem in Terris*, no. 60, National Catholic Welfare Conference ed. (Vatican Polygot Press).
25. Vatican Council II, *Gaudium et Spes*, no. 41.
26. Joseph Pieper, *The Four Cardinal Virtues* (Notre Dame: University of Notre Dame Press, 1966), p. 10.
27. St. Thomas Aquinas, *Summa Theologica*, II. II.Q48, A16.
28. Pieper, *The Four Cardinal Virtues*, p 161.
29. St. Thomas Aquinas, *Summa Theologica*, II. II.Q47, A14.
30. Ibid., II. II.Q47, A10, Reply Obj. 1.
31. Ibid., II. II.Q47, A10, Reply Obj. 2.
32. Allan Bloom, *The Closing of the American Mind: How Higher Education Has Failed Democracy and Impoverished the Souls of Today's Students* (New York: Simon & Schuster, 1987), p. 25.
33. Ibid., p. 34.
34. Ibid., pp. 82, 85.
35. Ibid., pp. 311–12.
36. Ibid., p. 42.
37. NCCB, *Economic Justice for All*, no. 33, p. 18.
38. Ibid., no. 34, pp. 18–19.
39. Ibid., no. 39, p. 22.
40. Ibid., no. 62, p. 33.
41. Ibid., nos. 12–22, pp. ix–xiii.
42. Ibid., no. 64, p. 33.
43. Ibid.
44. Ibid., no. 71, p. 36, citing Pope Pius XI, *Divine Redemptoris*, no. 51.
45. Ibid., no. 76, pp. 38–39.
46. Ibid., no. 77, p. 39.
47. Ibid., no. 78, p. 40.
48. Ibid., no. 86, p. 45.
49. Allan Bloom, *The Closing of the American Mind*, p. 119.
50. *Origins* 15, no. 27 (1985): 447.
51. Gregory the Great, *Pastoral Care* (New York: Newman Press, 1978), p. 68.
52. Ibid., p. 70.

3

Economic Justice and the Family

Allan C. Carlson

Today, perhaps as never before in its history, the American economy stands in need of a thoroughgoing critique from a family perspective. By virtue of its doctrines, history, and sheer size in America, the Roman Catholic Church is ideally suited to deliver that critique in the 1980s. Its apparent failure to meet that opportunity is something of a tragedy.

The system of liberal capitalism, which emerged over the course of the nineteenth century, attracted an array of critics, from scientific Marxists to conservative antimodernists. These critics differed on many points. Yet, significantly, they all agreed on one charge: that a labor and wage system constructed on market principles would, over time, undermine the family life.

Listen to one seemingly pro-family critic of capitalism from the nineteenth century. He described a situation in Yorkshire, England, where the rise of the factory system and the massive flow of married women into the paid labor force had turned many displaced men into house-husbands, sitting at home, darning their working wives' socks and caring for the children. "Can one imagine a more senseless and foolish state of affairs?" he wrote. "It deprives the husband of his manhood and the wife of all womanly qualities. Yet it cannot thereby turn a man into a woman or a woman into a man." The situation was "shameful and degrading," the corruption of the efforts of a hundred generations to improve the lot of humankind. "If all that can be achieved by our work and effort is this sort of mockery," the author concluded, "then we must truly despair of humanity and its aspirations."

Who was this reactionary, antifeminist critic? It was the young Friedrich Engels, later the co-founder with Karl Marx of modern communism. Together, they saw the family problem as among the central "contradictions of capitalism."

Others on the left have agreed. In this century, Swedish Social Democrats Alva and Gunnar Myrdal blasted capitalism for its failure to take account of family size and responsibility. Younger workers with small children, they noted, were usually the first to be laid off in a recession. Large families tended to live in the worst housing. In short, the Myrdals said, the incentive structure of modern capitalism imposed on most young couples a choice between poverty with children or a higher living standard without them.

Critics on the political right, such as the German antimodernist Roderich von Ungern-Sternberg, criticized the "striving spirit" of the middle class under capitalism. In the competitive race for success, he said, rational persons recognized that those with few or no children had a better chance of beating the competition. Industrial production, meanwhile, undermined the social and economic arrangements that had once given women "sensible occupations" in home production and management, and so discouraged the role of housewife and full-time mother.

Within the Catholic Church

A more measured criticism welled up within the Catholic church. It was Pope Leo XIII's 1891 social encyclical *Rerum Novarum* (On the Condition of Workers) that marked Catholicism's attempt to meet the promise and problems of industrialization with an alternative both to the laissez-faire doctrines of classical liberalism and to socialism. Arguing that "the present age handed over the workers, each alone and defenseless, to the inhumanity of employers and the unbridled greed of competitors," Leo rejected the wage theory of classical liberalism that considered that wage just which resulted from a free contract between employer and worker. Leo denied socialism with greater fervor, terming it "highly unjust" because it injured workers, violated the rights of lawful owners, perverted the functions of the state, and threw governments "into utter confusion." While arguing that humans, through the expenditure of mental energy and bodily strength in procuring natural goods, thereby appropriated to themselves the part of physical nature that they cultivated, Leo rejected both the rigid socialist labor theory of value and the standard socialist wage formulation— "from each according to his ability, to each according to his needs"—as inadequate.[1]

Instead, Leo turned to "the natural and primeval right of marriage" and to the family—"the society of the household"—as the proper foundation for social and economic theory. The right of ownership, for example, while bestowed on individuals by nature, was viewed as necessarily "assigned to man in his capacity as head of a family."[2] Similarly, Leo declared it "a most sacred law of nature that the father of a family see that his offspring are provided with all the necessities of life. . . ." In the natural order of life, he continued, it was not right "to demand of a woman or a child what a strong adult man is capable of doing or would be willing to do." Women, he affirmed, were "intended by nature for the work of the home . . . the education of children and the well-being of the family." Consequently, Leo concluded, the principle underlying all labor contracts must be that the wage be at least "sufficiently large to enable [the worker] to provide comfortably for himself, his wife, and his children." The moral wage and the Christian wage, he concluded, were the family wage.[3]

For several decades, though, the theological underpinnings of this concept remained fluid. For example, the Belgian Jesuit Valere Fallon continued during the 1920s to distinguish the family component of a worker's compensation from the wage itself. According to Fallon, a worker's market wage was the compensation received for his labor, while an extra family allowance was the amount paid to the worker by the employer and society to support his positions as father and family head.[4]

The 1930s, however, brought a refined theological understanding of the family-wage ideal. In his 1931 encyclical *Quadragesimo Anno* (Social Reconstruction), Pope Pius XI again affirmed that the first factor in determining a just wage was that the worker be paid sufficiently to support himself and his family. It was "an intolerable abuse . . . to be abolished at all costs," for mothers to be forced by their husbands' low wage to work outside the home, thereby neglecting their proper responsibilities, "especially the training of children." "Every effort must therefore be made," Pius concluded, to ensure "that fathers of families receive a wage large enough to meet ordinary family needs adequately." Social justice, he affirmed, demanded that reforms be introduced "without delay" to guarantee every adult working man just such a wage. He then rendered "merited praise to all, who with a wise and useful purpose have tried and tested various ways of adjusting the pay for work to family burdens in such a way that, as these increase, the [wage] may be raised and indeed, if the contingency arises, there may be enough to meet extraordinary needs."[5]

Reflecting this papal support, the 1930s and 1940s saw a flowering of treatises on the family-wage concept. Writing in the United States, for example, Jesuit scholar Daniel Callahan emphasized that the possession of property—including capital—was "contingent upon the superior rights of the workers to live and develop normally." He saw evidence of corruption and social decay in instances of child labor and where mothers were forced to work "to the neglect of their own proper cares and duties."[6]

More than a matter of charity or redistributive justice, Father Callahan continued, the family wage was an aspect of the natural law, an act of "commutative justice," and a "right" necessitated by the inherent duties of a father. Marriage and the begetting of children, Callahan noted, were necessary aspects of God's divine order. The purpose of human labor, moreover, was to secure the means of family sustenance. Hence the reward paid for adult human labor must be sufficient to meet that natural need. The unity of human fertility and the "fertility" of work, he stated, was implicit in the natural law. "The ideal to be aimed at is the acknowledgement of *per se* familial fertility in human labor, and its familial remuneration by a direct exercise of commutative justice."[7] He concluded that employers had a "strict obligation" to pay a family wage; that workers were justified in joining labor unions in order to secure such remuneration; and that the state must ensure that this natural right of laborers be secured through remedial and preventive legislation.[8]

Linking Work and Family Today

In his 1981 encyclical *Laborem Exercens* (On Human Work), Pope John Paul II reemphasized this necessary linkage of work and family. He asserted that the just wage for the work of an adult responsible for a family is that "which will suffice for establishing and properly maintaining a family and for providing security for its future." John Paul said that such compensation could be made through a pure family wage or through some combination of social-policy measures such as family allowances or grants to mothers devoting themselves exclusively to their children. He stresses in a key passage that, however accomplished, such arrangements served as "a concrete means of verifying the justice of the whole socio-economic system" involved. Phrased another way, the "family wage" served as the central measure of a just economic order.[9]

Expanding on these themes in his *Apostolic Exhortation on the Family,* John Paul II again cited "the fundamental bond between work and the family." Emphasizing the complications raised by the modern women's movement, he argued consistent with previous interpretations that "society must be structured in such a way that wives and mothers are not in practice compelled to work outside the home, and that their families can live and prosper in a dignified way even when [mothers] themselves devote their full time to their own family." The natural justice of the family wage, it is clear, remains central to Catholic social and economic teaching.

This doctrine linking the family and the economy is more than an untried theory. It has had practical results. The history of modern social policy in France, for example, shows Catholic thinkers, laity, and pressure groups as the primary forces active in the successful campaign to create a French family-allowance system in the 1920s. Similar stories could be told of Belgium and Italy, among other lands.

In light of this rich history, *Economic Justice for All* poses a problem. Instead of placing the tension between the family and a modern economy at or near the center of its analysis, the letter relegates its discussion of family allowances to a single short footnote. Even its guarded call for an investigation of "a family allowance or a children's allowance" is presented solely as a possible method for welfare reform. Neither the broad nature of the family economic problem nor the theological underpinnings for the concept rooted in natural-law doctrine is even noted, let alone discussed.

The fact is that the United States could use—indeed, is in great need of—a good course in historic Catholic social teaching on the family wage. The dominant line of Anglo-American economic thought, for example, is notoriously weak on the place of the family in modern economy. Brilliant eighteenth- and nineteenth-century analysts such as Adam Smith, David Ricardo, John Stuart Mill, and Alfred Marshall largely avoided discussing the relationship between wages and family burden. The twentieth century has done little better. As the British social theorist Eleanor Rathbone once concluded: "if the population of Great Britain consisted entirely of adult . . . bachelors and spinsters, nearly the whole output of writers on economic theory during the past fifty years might remain as it was written."[10] Marriage and children were simply not noticed. With the exception of the years since 1975, the same conclusion could be reached for economic theory in the United States.

The dominant American political tradition is also weak in describing the place of the family in our society. This weakness derives from the heavy philosophical influence of the philosophers Thomas Hobbes and John Locke on American political and legal institutions. Hobbes, for example, attacked the notion that the family was a natural institution: the family merely represented the exercise of the power of parents over their weaker children, he said. Locke tried to paint a more human face on Hobbes's competitive society composed of free individuals, yet he was able to carve out only a very limited role for parents as partial caretakers of their young children.

In the face of this general failure of American economic and political theory to address family life, why then have we not had more evidence of family stress and decay in this country? Why has our family crisis been evident only since about 1960? Politically speaking, the primary reason was that, until recently, family law and policy were the exclusive reserves of the states. These have been less beholden to Lockean doctrine, and more compatible with "common-law" and "natural-law" traditions, which affirm the place of the family.

Economically, the tendency toward excessive individualism was tempered by the construction of an informal "family-wage" economy. Farsighted industrialists, for example, grew aware of the social importance of stabilizing family life and set wages accordingly. Organized labor argued that the fair wage was one that allowed an adult male worker to maintain a family in modest comfort. As a pro-labor newspaper in Cripple Creek, Colorado, editorialized in the late nineteenth century, the measure of a decent wage was one sufficient for a man "to keep his wife and children out of competition with himself." During the 1920s the standard of a fair wage usually cited was the amount needed to maintain a family of five. The United Mine Workers made their case for a wage increase in 1920 on this very issue. So did the Railway Workers in 1922. Craft workers, almost without exception, also pushed the argument that the cost of maintaining a family of five should constitute the minimum wage.

A necessary corollary to this form of family wage was a valuation of women's labor at a lower, "individual" level, the argument being that most male laborers had wives and children to support, while most female laborers supported only themselves. Indeed, female labor was commonly perceived as a threat to the whole social fabric, due to the male worker's fear that a woman's lesser family responsibilities would enable her to undersell him. Also sustaining this dual-level wage system were compulsory education, prohibitions on child labor, restrictions on home work, the special protections accorded female labor, and the cultural creation of "male" and "female" jobs, all of which worked to keep married women and children out of direct market competition with their husbands and fathers.

Such cultural and legal restraints kept the negative consequences of liberal capitalism in check, and so allowed the new economic system to flower, and its blessings—unprecedented opportunity, social mobility, the end of mass poverty, the creation of great wealth—to emerge.

Historical Flaws

Yet this informal approach to constructing a family wage had serious flaws, which later contributed to its downfall. To begin with, it was quite inefficient. Calculations showed that fewer than half of male workers, at any given time, actually had dependent children at home, and fewer than one-fifth had three or more. Calculations in 1925 by economist Paul Douglas showed that if all adult male workers were paid enough to maintain a family of five, it would mean paying for 48,000 fictitious dependents.[11]

Second, a family wage keyed to male labor overlooked the small but significant number of women who, through death or desertion, had total responsibility for the support of their children.

Third, and perhaps most important, this system rested on institutionalized inequality. If and when pressures to secure the full "rights of women" grew to a critical level, the informal American family wage would be extremely vulnerable.

A few nondoctrinaire feminists saw the dilemma. Writing in 1924, Eleanor Rathbone in *Family Allowances* divided the causes of male antagonism toward female workers into two categories. The first included "the age-long tradition of masculine domination" and "the inevitable resentment felt by vested interests" toward a new class of competitors, attitudes that she labeled "selfish" and "antisocial." Yet the second category of attitudes included "the conviction that men have a right to all the best paid jobs, because they have to support wives and children out of their pay" and "the fear that [working] women, because they have no wives, and children to support, can afford to take less . . . and so will undercut men." These attitudes, Rathbone said, "are *not* unreasonable and to a considerable extent are justified by facts." She concluded: "If women are to fight the two former motives, they must find some way of getting rid of the two latter."[12]

Unfortunately, those pushing for gender equality in the United States have not followed this advice. Passage of the Equal Pay Act of 1963, Title VII of the Civil Rights Act of 1964, and subsequent laws and regulatory interpretations have all but scuttled the informal American family-wage system. The contemporary push for "Equal Pay for Work of Comparable Worth" promises to end, directly or indirectly, the last pieces of the old system. Yet absolutely nothing has been done to compensate for the family's loss of economic protection.

The old system, despite its flaws, at least made some effort to link the social need for human reproduction to the reward for labor.

Today, as a society, we do almost nothing to recognize the special burden of children. And the consequences are evident: a high divorce rate, a declining first-marriage rate, a sharp decline in marital fertility, and serious distress among youth.

So what can we do?

The favored solution of most analysts of the problems has been the construction of a system of family allowances, where parental income is supplemented by an allowance paid to all families on a per-child basis. Such a system counters the efficiency problem by targeting extra income only for families with dependent children. In a similar way, it solves the problem raised by children who are economically dependent on mothers. It also skirts the equality issue.

The problem with allowance programs is their tendency to become submerged within the welfare state. When first constructed in France and Belgium, allowance schemes operated privately, usually on an industry-wide basis. Yet problems of equity between industries quickly brought the French and the Belgian allowance programs under state control. As parts of these nations' respective social-security systems, allowances have been paid for through progressive income taxation, which discourages extra work. The allowance programs must also compete for funding with other state entitlements, such as old-age pensions. Under budgetary pressures, the value of such benefits has tended to diminish. Moreover, state allowances subtly transform families into a dependent class.

An American Alternative

There is, or could be, an American alternative. It involves using a distinctively American form of social policy: amending the income-tax code for social ends. Three tax-policy changes would go far toward creating a workable modern family wage: (1) increase the value of the personal exemption, for children only, to $4,000 per child; (2) extend the existing maximum child-care credit to all parents with preschool children, rather than confining it simply to those using day care; and (3) create a refundable $500 tax credit for each minor currently claimed as an exemption, up to the total value of the taxpayer's payment of FICA tax.

There are many advantages to this approach. First, instead of raising everyone's taxes and turning families into a dependent class, it would simply allow families to keep more of what they earn privately. Second, this approach avoids opening the family up to bureaucratic manipulation for other ends. Third, these policies are gender-neutral and can accommodate any number of work and child-care arrangements. And fourth, this form of tax relief can be readily justified on the "ability-to-pay" argument.

The fate of the family should be at the center of America's economic debates. In fact, it is usually not even mentioned. We need to correct that deficiency. The rich heritage of Catholic social theory is an extremely valuable resource in our work to restore to health the family in America. It remains to be more fully developed than it has been by, but not only by, the Catholic bishops of this country.

Notes

1. *Two Basic Social Encyclicals* (Washington, D.C.: The Catholic University of America Press), 5–11.
2. Ibid., 15.
3. Ibid., 55–59.
4. Vallere Fallon, S. J., *Les Allocations Familiales En Belgigue et en France* (Bruxelles: Editions de la société d'Etudes Morales, Sociales et Juuridiques, 1926), 98.
5. Pope Pius XI, *Quadvagesimo Anno* in *Two Basic Social Encyclicals.* op. cit. 133–35.
6. John Daniel Callahan, S. J., *The Catholic Attitude Toward a Familial Minimum Wage* (Washington, D.C.: The Catholic University of America Press, 1936), 65–68.
7. Ibid., 97–98.
8. Ibid., 127–28.
9. Pope John Paul II, *Laborem Exercens,* St. Paul Editions, Vatican translation, 46.
10. Eleanor Rathbone, *Family Allowances* (London: George Allen and Unwin, 1924).
11. Paul Douglas, *Wages and the Family* (Chicago: University of Chicago Press, 1925), ix.
12. Rathbone, *Family Allowances.*

4

Facts, Credibility, and the Bishops' Economic Views

J. Peter Grace

The final draft of the Catholic bishops' Pastoral Letter on the economy showed no evidence that they had changed their basic views since they issued their first draft more than a year and a half earlier. They continued to urge more government involvement in the economy, ignoring the trend of more than five years in both the United States and Europe, where countries were lowering the growth rate of government spending (including social programs) in an effort to improve economic performance.

An appendix to the letter lists those who testified before the bishops' committee. Although a fairly wide diversity of economic opinion is evident among those who testified before the issuance of the first draft in November 1984, the only world-class economist to testify after that was John Kenneth Galbraith, the Harvard liberal, who was economic adviser to Presidents Franklin D. Roosevelt, John F. Kennedy, and Lyndon B. Johnson.

The bishops write convincingly about the relevance of religion and the Bible to economics, the dignity of serving the poor, the hedonistic consumerism of American society, the need for ethical standards to guide the economic conduct of institutions, managers, investors, and workers (this made even more relevant by recent scandals in the investment banking and brokerage fields), and the right of an individual to participate with dignity in developing his or her talents. They can also be applauded for their broad comments on the skewed distribution of wealth in the United States and between the United States and the developing countries.

When the bishops move to specific policy recommendations, however, they lose their moral tone, their message sounding more like a legislative agenda prepared for Lyndon Johnson than a group of clerics calling attention to the moral, religious, and ethical dimension of the society they want to change. For example, in their comments on welfare reform, the bishops declare that public assistance programs should have national eligibility standards and a national minimum-benefit level. They write:

> Currently welfare eligibility and benefits vary greatly among states. In 1985 a family of three with no earnings had a maximum AFDC [Aid to Families with Dependent Children] benefit of $96 a month in Mississippi and $558 a month in Vermont. To remedy these great disparities, which are far larger than the regional differences in the cost of living, and to assure a floor of benefits for all needy people, our nation should establish and fund national minimum-benefit levels and eligibility standards in cash-assistance programs. The benefits should also be indexed to reflect changes in the cost of living.[1]

This proposal, however well intentioned, ignores evidence that there is a positive correlation between AFDC benefits and poverty rates, as follows. Between 1969 and 1979 the average poverty rate *increased* by 4.0 percent (from 9.9 percent to 10.3 percent) in the ten states with the highest AFDC benefits. The poverty rate for children under age eighteen increased 36.0 percent in these states, going from 10.0 percent to 13.6 percent. Monthly AFDC benefits averaged $282 per family in these states in 1975, 28.8 percent more than the $219 per family average for the nation.

On the other hand, the ten *lowest-spending* states (average AFDC benefit of $104 per family in 1975, 52.5 percent below the national average) experienced sharply *lower poverty* over the 1969–79 period. The average poverty rate in these states declined by 26.5 percent, from 23.1 percent in 1969 to 17.0 percent in 1979, while the poverty rate for children under age eighteen fell 18.9 percent, from 26.5 percent to 21.5 percent.

This trend is consistent with the idea, proposed by Charles Murray in his book *Losing Ground,* that overgenerous welfare payments create additional poverty by inducing workers to give up low-paying jobs voluntarily in order to qualify for transfer payments. According to Murray, this explains much of the increase in the U.S. poverty rate during the late 1970s and early 1980s, despite record levels of real per-capita federal welfare payments.

Although the bishops acknowledge that some social programs do not work as intended, they imply that this failure is primarily due to insufficient funding, rather than to basic flaws inherent to these programs.

A recent study by two Ohio University economists, Lowell Gallaway and Richard Vedder, indicated, for example, that the financial incentives built into federal welfare programs make having children out of wedlock a rational, economically beneficial decision. Until a poor child reaches age twelve, the annual welfare benefits (AFDC and food stamps) associated with the child exceed the annual costs of raising the child.[2]

Average welfare benefits exceed the average cost of an additional child by $598 in the child's first year of life, and remain above $550 per year until age four. Over the seventeen-year period, the female-headed family can expect total welfare benefits to exceed the total cost of raising the child by $3,391—$25,740 in benefits vs. $22,249 in costs. According to these economists, poor families are given, in effect, a $3,207 lump-sum grant over and above the costs of raising each additional child.

This amount probably *underestimates* the true net welfare benefits from having children because: *(a)* poverty children often leave the household before their eighteenth birthday, *(b)* no account is taken of the additional tax exemption for the poor child if the family pays income taxes, and *(c)* no account is taken of income the children might earn before age eighteen.

The bishops urge antipoverty policies that "support the strength and stability of families," warning that "the high rate of divorce and the alarming extent of teen-age pregnancies in our nation are distressing signs of the breakdown of traditional family values." Yet the increase in the U.S. divorce rate also has been linked to the perverse incentives of the AFDC program, which, until recently, was available in many states only to poor families with children but no husband present.

Starting in the late 1960s the divorce rate skyrocketed beyond the range of 1.6 to 2.8 per 1,000 population, within which it had been since these data were first collected in the 1920s. From 1965—the beginning of the War on Poverty—until 1979, the divorce rate more than doubled, rising from 2.5 to 5.3 divorces per 1,000.[3] The same period saw a 55.6 percent rise in the percentage of poor people living in families headed by females—from 33.3 percent in 1965 to 51.8 percent in 1979.[4] Thus far in the 1980s, both the divorce rate and the percentage of poor living in female-headed families have declined slightly.

Gallaway and Vedder's model shows that more than 50 percent of the increase in the U.S. divorce rate since 1965 is explainable by the growth in welfare spending. Approximately 300,000 of the 1.2 million divorces occurring annually in the late 1970s are attributable to the growth in real welfare benefits. Overall, it is estimated that every additional $1 of per-capita aid results in 5,000 more families headed by females. According to these Ohio economists, these results are strong evidence against those who believe the relationship between the rising divorce rate and increases in welfare payments is merely a coincidence, or that increases in the divorce rate may cause the increased welfare, rather than vice versa.

Unfortunately, public policy is still strongly influenced by those (such as the bishops) who for one reason or another choose to play down the evidence linking increased poverty to increased welfare. A bill entitled the "Omnibus Anti-Poverty Act of 1984" would, if it had passed, have mandated minimum AFDC benefits for the states, forcing forty-one of them to raise their benefit levels by 1986. At the extreme, Mississippi would have been forced to more than quadruple its AFDC benefits for a family of three. (Mississippi's poverty rate declined 32.5 percent, going from 35.4 percent to 23.9 percent, between 1969 and 1979, the largest percentage decline among the ten states that had the lowest AFDC benefits in 1975.) If Congress had set out deliberately to increase the rate of poverty among children it could have done no better than this legislation. What is required, instead, is a restructuring of incentives so that the potential poverty population is encouraged—as well as enabled—to avoid poverty in the first place.

Regarding specific points of the bishops' letter:

In April 1986 nearly half—49.5 percent—of the 8.1 million unemployed were unemployed because they either left their jobs, reentered the labor force, or were new entrants to the labor force. Only 50.5 percent of the unemployed were unemployed because they lost their jobs:

TABLE 4.1
Reasons for Unemployment
April 1986

	1 Number of Unemployed (In Thousands)	2 Percentage of Total	3 Percentage of Civilian Labor Force
1. Job losers	4,095,000	50.4	3.5
2. Job leavers	996,000	12.3	0.9
3. Reentrants	2,042,000	25.2	1.8
4. New Entrants	982,000	12.1	0.8
5. Total	8,115,000	100.0	7.0

Source: Bureau of Labor Statistics

If one considers job leavers and reentrants to be voluntarily unemployed, as in a sense they are, then the true number of unemployed falls to 5,077 million, comprised of 4,095 million job losers and 982,000 million new labor-force entrants, and the unemployment rate falls to 4.3 percent instead of the official 7.0 percent.

Although the bishops rank unemployment as the most crucial economic problem confronting the country, in reality the increase in the civilian labor force and in the number of employed, both in absolute numbers and as a percentage of the population, has been remarkable. It was remarkable at the time the bishops wrote, and it has continued well into 1989.

Total civilian employment was a record 108.9 million in April 1986, when the bishops were writing, compared to only 58.9 million in 1950, that is, 50 million new jobs created since 1950, of which more than 9 million were created since 1982.

The labor-force participation rate (labor force as a percentage of civilian population aged sixteen and over) was at a record 65.1 percent in April 1986. It has risen 10.0 percent (5.9 percentage points) since 1950, with most of the growth occurring since 1975. Civilian employment as a percentage of the civilian population was also at a record 60.5 percent in April 1986, up 8.0 percent from the 56.0 percent level of 1975. It has continued to increase since then.

These numbers attest to the underlying strength of the U.S. economy, which has successfully absorbed the influx of baby boomers into the labor force. Yet the bishops call for increased government support for direct job-creation programs, which have, for the most part, been expensive failures.

The bishops blame high rates of joblessness among racial minorities and women on "discrimination," conveniently ignoring an alternative explanation, namely, that misguided public policies such as the minimum wage contribute to this situation. The bishops, by focusing on the unemployment rate, miss the big picture of record employment levels in this country.

The bishops indicate that 2 percent of the families own 28 percent of the total net wealth and the top 10 percent hold 57 percent of the net wealth. They also said that 54 percent of the total net financial assets were held by 2 percent of all families, those whose annual income is over $125,000, and that 86 percent of these assets were held by the top 10 percent of all families.

The numbers on the distribution of wealth and financial assets cited by the bishops are those reported in the Federal Reserve Board's "Survey of Consumer Finances, 1983: A Second Report," which was released in December 1984. A footnote to the Federal Reserve's survey indicates, however, that the net-worth data exclude the value of consumer durables such as automobiles and home furnishings, and the value of small businesses and farms. In other words, the survey that the bishops rely upon to show how unequally wealth is distributed in the United States does not count those assets that account for a large share of family net worth in this country.

Moreover, the Federal Reserve survey reports that the distribution of *income* is much less uneven than the distribution of assets: only 14 percent of total income is received by the highest 2 percent of families, and 33 percent by the top 10 percent. These numbers reflect the distribution of pre-tax income only, thereby ignoring the effect of the progressive income tax.

The present level of inequality, both within this country and between the United States and the less developed countries (LCDs), is deemed "unacceptable" by the bishops. However, all industrial and industrializing societies—whether capitalist, socialist, or communist—exhibit patterns of economic inequality. They would have been better off judging the absolute rather than the relative standard of living of the poor, and if such a criterion were applied to American society (or to any other industrialized, capitalist nation), the bishops would find the condition of the poor in America to rank among the highest in human history.

Even so, the bishops' zeal for increased economic equality leads them to recommend tax reform. They write:

> Those with relatively greater financial resources should pay a higher rate of taxation—both in principle and in the actual or "effective" tax rates paid. The inclusion of such a principle in tax policies is an important means of reducing the severe inequalities of income and wealth in the nation.[5]

As with their pronouncements on welfare, the bishops' tax policy reveals a fundamental misunderstanding of how economic incentives work. The experience of the past few years shows that lowering, not raising, tax rates on the rich is the proper tax policy for those interested in increasing the share of taxes paid by the wealthy (see Table 4.2).[6]

Income taxes paid by the wealthiest 1 percent of taxpayers rose by 25.1 percent between 1981 and 1984, taxes paid by the top 5 percent rose 19.0 percent, while taxes paid by the bottom 95 percent actually declined by 1.0 percent. During this period marginal tax rates were cut by approximately 23 percent for most income levels, while top-bracket taxpayers saw their rates cut by 28.6 percent on both capital gains (from 28 percent to 20 percent) and other nonwage income (from 70 percent to 50 percent).

In other words, the 1981–84 tax cut resulted in greater relative and absolute tax payments by high-income taxpayers, even though in many cases they received a larger tax cut than others.

The increased tax burden on the wealthy obviously cannot be explained by changes in tax rates per se but, rather, by the response of taxpayers to tax-rate changes, that is, investing more in taxable activities and less in tax shelters. The experience of 1981–84 shows that far more income is now taxed at a 50 percent rate than was taxed at rates that previously went as high as 70 percent. Clearly, those concerned with income distribution must look beyond statutory or effective tax rates to the amount of income actually taxed at those rates.

TABLE 4.2
Income Taxes Paid
by Adjusted Gross Income Group
($ billions)

	1 Wealthiest 1 percent	2 Wealthiest 5 percent	3 Bottom 95 percent	4 Total
1. 1981	$51.0	$98.6	$183.7	$282.3
2. 1982	53.6	99.5	176.6	276.1
3. 1983	54.1	101.1	170.5	271.6
4. 1984	63.8	117.3	181.8	299.1
5. % increase 1981–84	**25.1 percent**	19.0 percent	**(1.0) percent**	6.0 percent
		% Of Total		
6. 1981	18.1	34.9	65.1	100.0
7. 1982	19.4	36.0	64.0	100.0
8. 1983	19.9	37.2	62.8	100.0
9. 1984	21.3	39.2	60.8	100.0
10. 1984 as Multiple of 1981	1.2x	1.1x	0.9x	1.0x

In brief, the bishops' letter continues to point to governmental intervention as the ultimate provider and guarantor of all good. America did not reach its economic peak by the actions of a benevolent government. The same private sector that raised our standard of living must be trusted to continue to produce the benefits that the bishops feel are the rights of all individuals. History has not produced a government that can produce more benefits for more people than the private sector has. The bishops have not seen fit to recognize this and, because of that, their Pastoral Letter lacks credibility.

Notes

1. National Conference of Catholic Bishops (NCCB), *Economic Justice for All: Pastoral Letter on Catholic Social Teaching and the U.S. Economy* (Washington, D.C.: USCC, 1986), no. 210.
2. See data in "Suffer the Little Children: The True Casualties of the War on Poverty," by Lowell Gallaway and Richard Vedder, Economics Department, University of Ohio. The study was reprinted in a Joint

Economic Committee publication on a "War on Poverty—Victory or Defeat?" hearing of June 20, 1985, pp. 48–63.

3. U.S. Department of Commerce, *Historical Statistics of the U.S.,* and *Statistical Abstract of the U.S.,* various years.

4. U.S. Bureau of the Census, *Money Income and Poverty Status of Families and Persons in the U.S.: 1984.*

5. NCCB, *Economic Justice for All,* no. 199.

6. Internal Revenue Service, as reported in *Tax Notes* of June 9, 1986, p. 1029.

5

The Future of "Economic Rights"

Michael Novak

One of the important tasks before the Catholic church is to clarify its teaching on "economic rights." No doubt, in *Pacem in Terris* the Catholic church does recognize at least two different types of "economic rights." It recognizes the same type of civil rights in economic matters recognized in the U.S. Constitution: rights to private property, initiative, and responsibility, for example. (*Pacem in Terris* leaves out one important economic right, the right of authors and inventors to the fruit of their discoveries, for a limited time, as defined in the U.S. Constitution, art. 1, sec. 8.)

The other type of "right" spoken of in *Pacem in Terris* is called by the editors of some English translations "rights to life" or "welfare rights," that is, rights to the material goods necessary to human life, such as food, shelter, medical care, security in old age, and so forth. Disputation arises, however, over the precise meaning of the word "rights" in paragraph 11 of *Pacem in Terris*.

In their Pastoral Letter on the U.S. economy (no. 80), the U.S Catholic bishops seem to interpret *Pacem in Terris* (no. 11) to mean that every human being, just by virtue of being human, has a "right" (claim) to food, clothing, shelter, and so forth. Others, including myself, argue that every able-bodied person has a *responsibility* to provide these necessary means for self and dependents; however, when through no fault of his or her own a person cannot meet that responsibility, then, by virtue of being made in the image of God, each person has a claim upon support from others. In paragraphs 79–84 in their Pastoral Letter on the U.S. economy, the U.S. bishops *seem* to make the claim to welfare benefits universal, belonging to "all persons."

The opposing view is that welfare rights are *conditional*. Able-bodied persons do *not* have a right to be dependent upon others, *unless* through no fault of their own they cannot meet their own responsibilities. Otherwise, human persons would be held to be neither independent nor responsibile. To suggest that human persons are universally and necessarily dependent on others, society, or the state for their material necessities is to ignore the very ground of their liberty and their dignity. It is clear from other texts in the Pastoral Letter that the bishops *do* hold persons responsibile for meeting their own needs, if they can. In that case, though, they should have been more careful in their wording concerning economic rights. In practice, they view welfare rights as conditional; but their initial formulation did not express that clearly.

Wording is very important here, but not solely as a verbal matter. Words belong to intellectual traditions, and swiftly lose their meaning if their original context is suddenly switched. A few changes in fundamental concepts can have profound and lasting consequences, which need to be carefully inspected in advance.

For some years, David Hollenbach, S.J., the primary drafter of the philosophical sections of the Pastoral Letter, has called upon the Catholic church to synthesize the liberal tradition of human rights and the Marxist tradition. He described his project in *Claims in Conflict:*

> Liberal democracy notes that not all are willing to have society guarantee social and economic rights and concludes that these rights are not really rights at all. Rights are identified with claims to political liberty. Marxism, on the other hand, notes that unrestricted liberty in a society stratified according to classes leads to a denial of social and economic rights. Political liberty must be restricted if social and economic claims are to be guaranteed. Thus Soviet Marxism has concluded that political and civil rights exist only as grants from the state. . . . The valid contributions and the limitations of both theories we have been examining suggest that a theory incorporating both perspectives is called for. The urgent need is for a theory of political institutions built on the principle of respect of both sets of claims. . . . The human rights debate, both in the United States and internationally, is in essence a debate about the possibility of creating such a new ideology.[1]

My experience at the Human Rights Commission of the United Nations and as U.S. ambassador to the meeting of the Helsinki Process in Bern have taught me that such a project has dangerous possibilities. To the one side, it risks cheapening and misconstruing the "liberal" tradition of political and civil rights. (In the United States, at least, the farmers are far more accurately placed in the "Whig" tradition, which has roots in Aristotle, Cicero, and Thomas Aquinas—a point of great significance.) To the other side, it risks blindness to the latent function of Marxist declarations of economic rights, which is to keep individuals thoroughly dependent upon the state in every economic activity.

Nonetheless, the questions involved in this discussion are complex. The *aim* of all parties to the debate is to be sure that citizens who are able act responsibly and that citizens unable to help themselves receive the necessary assistance. The *end* is not in dispute. In dispute are the means, the method, and the intellectual conception of social *order*. Since this argument is an important one, and rather complex, it is probably better to unpack its elements patiently one by one. Thus the U.S. bishops write in their Pastoral Letter (no. 84): "There is certainly room for diversity of opinion in the church and in U.S. society on *how* to protect the human dignity and economic rights of all our brothers and sisters. In our view, however, there can be no legitimate disagreement on the basic moral *objectives*" (italics added). In this passage, the bishops seem to be saying that their conception of rights is a matter of goals, ends, objectives.

With this in mind, I would like to examine the different ways in which Hollenbach and I regard the status of "economic rights." Hollenbach disagreed with a text of mine in which I insisted upon the essential differences between two distinct realities—between "rights" to civil and political liberties, on the one hand, and the material "good" (such as food, shelter, medical care) necessary to life. My actual sentences read as follows.

In short, the true conceptual force of the argument in favor of economic rights (to income, food, shelter, a job, etc.) is *not* that the latter are truly "rights" inhering in the nature of human persons, but rather that they are "goods" indispensable to a full human life. Since at present levels of economic development such goods are within human power to provide, one can say unambiguously that they ought in justice to be provided. The bearers of the primary responsibility for providing them however, are individuals in mature independence and self-reliance; secondarily, human communities and associations; and only *in extremis,* the state. Human persons ought not be wards of the state. They ought not to be dependent. They ought not to be servile. Nothing less than mature independence and self-reliance is becoming to the dignity of human persons.[2]

Father Hollenbach finds it "impossible to see how one could reasonably say, from a moral point of view, that the avoidance of hunger, homelessness and chronic unemployment is part of a 'full human life' while democratic freedoms are somehow more basic. From my perspective they both look equally fundamental."[3]

Perhaps this is a matter of experience. When I was a child, I do not remember hunger but I do remember the bread my mother put into hamburger to stretch it, many meals of beans or rice (served in many forms), hours of canning home-grown vegetables "to get through the winter," and so forth. My aunt Emma and her husband lived in a shack on the highway outside of town, and took in homeless youths and indigent wayfarers. My grandfather was out of work (my uncle had to quit the university), and gratefully accepted, although not as a "right," assistance in the form of Works Progress Administration (WPA) employment. In the mills and mines of the Johnstown area unemployment was then (as it is now) chronic. All of my relatives had come to these shores hungry, homeless, and unemployed. But they were now *free*.

Not only were these realities distinct in their lives, they knew which one was the more fundamental, inviolable, and endowed in them by the Creator, and which one was first of all their own responsibility. Further, they knew that with freedom a healthy man and woman could find ways to work, to grow their own food, and to build their own shelter. Freedom is not only a more basic right. It is also the best means for meeting one's own responsibilities to earn one's own food, shelter, and employment, thus achieving the dignity of financial independence.

Hollenbach's argument—that political and civil rights are "fundamentally equal" to economic rights—has three equivalents in international discourse today. All three are part of the international context in which the bishops' Pastoral Letter is being read. (1) The

Soviets say that their human-rights record is at least equal to that of the United States, because they meet all the economic rights. (2) Cubans say their people might not be free, but they are not hungry. (3) The quip of Anatole France is often quoted: "Both the poor man and the rich man have a right to sleep under the bridge." Each of these has an appropriate response.

1. Maurice Cranston has observed that "economic and social rights" were inserted in the U.N. Declaration on Human Rights "under pressure from the Soviet Union and its allies, who could hardly pretend to uphold the individual's right to liberty and property. . . ."[4] Leszek Kolakowski has written that "[W]hen Soviet ideologists speak of human rights, they invariably stress that the chief human right is the right to work, and that this has been granted under the Soviet system only. What they fail to add is that this has been achieved by a system of compulsory labor that was established in principle at the very beginning of Sovietism. Thus the supreme right of man and his supreme freedom are materialized in the form of slavery."[5]

2. It was no defense of slavery in the Confederacy to say: "But our slaves are well fed."

3. It is not good that the poor should sleep under a bridge, but it is even worse for the poor to be subject to arbitrary arrest and to being sent to forced labor camps. It is demeaning to the poor to think that they care about liberty less than the rich. Since the days of Anatole France, moreover, millions of poor have fled to free nations, even at the cost of arriving penniless, homeless, unemployed—and even without knowing a word of the local tongue.

The second argument Hollenbach makes against me is fashioned around John Courtney Murray's distinction of "public order" and "common good." That distinction works well in matters of religious liberty and freedom of speech. It does not work equally well for rights to food, shelter, and the like—which is why I did not use it. Hollenbach, nonetheless, suggests that I did use it: "Novak suggests that providing basic economic necessities is part of the obligation to promote the common good (the fullness of human flourishing), but not part of the obligation to protect public order (the minimal conditions for social coexistence)." I never drew that distinction. Nonetheless, Hollenbach then writes: "It is on the strength of this distinction that Novak's brief against economic rights rises or falls. He will hardly be surprised to learn that I think it falls.'' I am not surprised that this argument was *designed* to fall, only that it is attributed to me.

Hollenbach recognizes that I fully support welfare payments to the needy, either to help them to regain their economic autonomy (and full dignity), if they can, or to nourish them well in their dependency, if they cannot. Then he adds:

> If government's proper sphere is public order and not the common good, and if, as Novak appears to believe, the provision of basic economic resources is part of the full common good rather than part of the more basic condition of public order, then it makes no sense to sanction any intervention at all. Novak's refusal to go this far shows that there is a basic flaw in his argument. And that flaw is his refusal to admit that economic rights exist. Or is his real agenda to delegitimate the role of government in securing human welfare altogether?[6]

That last line is a cheap shot, not typical of Hollenbach. My writings on the legitimacy of the welfare function are unambiguous. The Lay Letter *Toward the Future* also supplies sound arguments for the welfare function.

Curiously, though, the same argument that Hollenbach uses against me in fact impales him. He holds that ''government's proper sphere is public order and not the common good.'' He wishes to assert that ''the provision of basic economic resources'' is part of ''public order.'' He seems to believe that it is necessary to choose an either/or: *either* public order *or* the common good. In that way, he thinks that I am impaled on the horns of a dilemma. But the exact dilemma impales him. If he believes that ''economic rights'' fall solely under ''public order,'' why, in that case, does he insist that the first responsibility for providing for one's basic needs inheres in oneself, the second in one's communities and mediating structures, and only as a last resort in the state? Why, in a lecture at the American Enterprise Institute in 1985, did Archbishop Rembert G. Weakland say of ''economic rights'' that ''the whole of society''—not the state—''guarantees these rights''? ''Economic rights'' involve much more than ''public order'' or the state.

The truth is that here there is no either/or. The people of the United States in establishing their government, as stated explicitly in the Preamble to the Constitution, did so in order to ''ensure justice" and "promote the general welfare." There are some things that government can legitimately do to promote the achievement of the common good in many dynamic ways that are consistent with, but go beyond, concerns for mere "public order." And it can do these things without infringing upon liberties, without ceasing to base its actions upon the "consent of the governed," and without transgressing the bounds of limited government. Among such people-empowering actions by our own government might be cited the Homestead Act, the land-grant colleges, the Highway Act, rural electrification, the Social Security Act, food stamps, housing assistance, AFDC (Aid to Families with Dependent Children), and a host of others. To justify these, one does not need a doctrine of "economic rights" or "welfare rights."

In short, "economic rights" cannot be squeezed solely into Murray's concept of "public order." In fact, any state that is pledged to recognize "economic rights" to food, shelter, income, and so forth, for all persons, not only for the smaller class of individuals in need, would soon cease to be a limited state. Maurice Cranston has pointed out that "economic rights" accepted for the smaller class of those in need are less than universal and less than inalienable.

Finally, Hollenbach urged me to consult John Courtney Murray's essay, "Two Concepts of Government." So I looked again at that essay, only to discover on the very page Hollenbach cites that Murray agrees with me. Murray places "the special function of government with regard to the disinherited masses" under the heading of the "common good":

> If one wished to sum up [Pope] Leo's political concept of government in its relation to the socio-economic order, one might well use the phrase, "As much freedom as possible, as much government as necessary. . . ." The general principle upon which it is based is extremely broad—the obligations of government to the common good and to the social values which are common goods, such as justice, freedom, a due measure of equality, public prosperity and peace, etc. The applications of the principle are subject to the canons of political prudence.[7]

Murray describes Pope Leo XIII's vision as intermediate between the Enemy on the left (the principle of interventionism) and the

Enemy on the right ("free enterprise" alone, or libertarianism). That is the same intermediate position that informs the Lay Letter *Toward the Future,* as well as all my own work. It is a vision of *political economy;* it gives to both polity and economy legitimate, intersecting roles.

It is useful to note, nonetheless, that *operationally* Hollenbach's position and mine are almost identical. He writes:

> Both Leo XIII and Murray insisted, of course, that securing economic necessities for all is not, in the first instance, the responsibility of government. Individuals, families and a variety of mediating institutions in society have an obligation to see that people do not go hungry, homeless or jobless. Nevertheless, when the problem exceeds the power of these persons and groups, government can and should intervene in ways carefully guided by political prudence.[8]

Unlike Hollenbach, it is true, I distinguish among six of the many senses of the word "right": (1) its sense as a rhetorical intensifier; (2) its Catholic sense; (3) its legal sense in the United States; (4) its constitutional sense; (5) its philosophical sense in Anglo-American usage; (6) its Marxist and socialist senses. In addition to (3) and (4), I accept "economic rights" in sense (2), the Catholic sense, rooted in the virtue of justice and in the shared dignity of all persons as children of God, redeemed by Christ. This second meaning, the Catholic meaning, is distinct from the other five meanings, and its distinctiveness should be defended.

Following Pope John XXIII in *Pacem in Terris* (par. 11), I believe it is vitally important to distinguish between "welfare rights," which are conditional, and the specific "economic rights" mentioned later in *Pacem in Terris* (pars. 18–22), which are already protected in the U.S. Constitution and Bill of Rights. Not only are "welfare rights" not "rights" in the full sense, and not only are they conditional (being first responsibilities, and claims upon others only under certain conditions); they are better to be described in terms of objectives, ends, *goals*—that is, as highly important social goals, part of the "general welfare."

Operationally, nonetheless, I come out where Hollenbach comes out. Speaking of welfare rights in this sense, I write:

> The primary responsibility for meeting his own/her own basic needs is invested in the individual person; secondly, in mediating human asso-

ciations and social organizations; thirdly, only as a last resort and with a wary and critical eye, in the state.[9]

These two texts from Hollenbach and myself seem to put us operationally on common ground.

The third draft of the bishops' Pastoral Letter reflected this common ground, even though it failed to distinguish unmistakably between the two very different meanings of the word "rights"— one reflecting genuine, universal political and civil rights (even in the economic order) and the other reflecting conditional rights that fall under the "general welfare" and the "common good."

Further, in his *America* article Hollenbach made several helpful advances beyond the first draft of the Pastoral Letter. First, he made clear that the bishops did not mean by "economic rights" a new set of *constitutional* amendments. Second, they did not mean a new set of *legal* rights; means and methods of achieving "objectives" would be left open. Third, the bishops intended that declarations of economic rights should keep the principle of limited government intact. That is, economic rights must be kept consistent with political and civil rights and not, as in Marxist thought, substitutes for political and civil rights. Fourth, the bishops held that individuals bear the first responsibility for meeting their own minimum economic necessities; that other persons, communities, and mediating institutions bear the second line of responsibility for helping those who cannot help themselves; that only as a last resort does the government (local, state, or federal) bear such responsibility; and that government should meet this responsibility of being last, in Hollenbach's felicitous formulation, "in ways carefully guided by political prudence."

In the lecture at the American Enterprise Institute mentioned above, Archbishop Weakland summarized his understanding of economic rights: "We are saying that all have a right to contribute to the common good and we, thus, make the fulfillment of the basic needs of the poor the highest priority of any society." This also seems to be an argument from "common good" and "society," not from "public order" and "state."

The classic American documents attack this problem by stressing the role of property in enabling all citizens to meet their own basic needs and, more than that, to achieve unprecedented prosperity. Thus the Virginia Declaration of Rights affirmed in 1776 that all men are by nature equally free and independent, and have certain inherent rights, of which, when they enter a state of society, they cannot by any compact deprive or divest their posterity; namely, the enjoyment of life and liberty, with the means of acquiring and possessing property, and pursuing and obtaining happiness and safety.

In his First Inaugural Address, Thomas Jefferson described Americans as "entertaining a due sense of our equal right to the use of our own faculties, to the acquisitions of our own industry, to honor . . . resulting not from birth, but from our actions." And he asked: "With all these blessings, what more is necessary to make us a happy and a prosperous people?" His answer: "Still one thing more, fellow-citizens—a wise and frugal Government, which shall restrain men from injuring one another, shall leave them otherwise free to regulate their own pursuits of industry and improvement, and shall not take from the mouth of labor the bread it has earned."

In other words, the new republic would be constituted as a community of self-reliance. Self-reliance under law and liberty would be the original contribution of the American proposition to the age-old human question of how to overcome poverty and basic economic needs. True, humans have a right to life and to all the things necessary to sustain life. Government ought not to take away these rights, nor take from citizens the bread they have earned. Free citizens have the primary responsibility, in liberty and under law, to fulfill these rights. In *Pacem in Terris,* Pope John XXIII seemed to capture this American idea very well:

> The dignity of the human person also requires that every man enjoy the rights freely and responsibly. For this reason, in social relations especially man should exercise his rights, fulfill his obligations and, in the countless forms of collaboration with others, act chiefly on his own responsibility and initiative. This is to be done in such a way that each one acts on his own decision, of set purpose and from a consciousness of his obligation, without being moved by force or pressure brought to bear on him externally. For any human society that is established on the sole basis of force must be regarded as simply inhuman, inasmuch as the freedom of its members is repressed, when in fact they should be provided with appropriate incentives and means for developing and perfecting themselves.[10]

Free citizens have a right not only to live but to live with that degree of virtue necessary for maintaining a free society. They have the further right to pursue a life far above the mere level of subsistence or "basic needs," a right to pursue "prosperity" and "felicity." Government can provide opportunity but not success. For those in need, it can also provide assistance.

Thus, for example, in cases of natural catastrophe—flood, tornado, hurricane, and so forth—the state legitimately acts quickly to send in the National Guard, to establish shelters in public buildings, to cooperate with the Red Cross and other organizations in rapidly supplying medicines, foods, and bedding, and to provide disaster relief. In cases of massive unemployment, the Congress has often in the past established various programs of "relief." Consent to a whole panoply of "social welfare" legislation has also been favored by massive majorities among the American people. To care for the needy and the vulnerable among us, the American state has been more generous in the last two decades than at any previous time in American history. No doubt, more can be done and what has been done can be done better. In order to support both public and private agencies to meet such needs, however, it is not necessary to declare new "economic rights."

In the sound Catholic sense, though, one can insist that when the citizens of a liberal (or "Whig") society such as our own come to the assistance of the poor and the vulnerable in their midst, through governmental programs (where prudent and truly helpful), they do so not out of charity but out of justice: recognizing the fundamental equality of each in the eyes of the Creator of all. It is not paternalistic for a free government to help the needy. But it would become so were such assistance unintentionally to generate the dependency characteristic of what Hilaire Belloc called "the servile society," and Alexis de Tocqueville called the "new, soft despotism." To make the needy dependent upon the state is not to enhance their dignity. For that reason—as the Pastoral Letter also seems to assert at several places—Catholic social thought calls upon the state as a last resort, one hopes in a temporary way, and insists upon personal responsibility.

Again it should be noted that Hollenbach tended in 1985 to inflate the concept of "minimum economic necessities" or "basic needs." The family meals we ate during the Great Depression certainly met our "basic needs," but if they were established as a standard "basic minimum" for poor people today, I think there would be many loud and angry protests. On the other hand, the meals we had in our home when I was a child would probably seem not "basic" but luxurious to many a poor person in other nations today. In the United States, standards of poverty are set so far above "basic needs," "minimum economic necessities," or "subsistence" that the use of such concepts can only be extremely analogical. United States definitions of poverty are set very far above the level of subsistence or basic needs, deliberately so and appropriately so. They should also be constantly revised upward, as they are. The woman who established these measures for the federal government, Mollie Orshansky, knew in this respect exactly what she was doing.

The crucial point is that the drafters of the third draft of the Pastoral Letter did clarify the paragraphs on economic rights appearing in the first and second drafts. Except for one thing. They still did not mark out the crucial differences between the various senses in which they use the word "rights." A consensus faithful both to Catholic social thought and to the American Proposition is within reach, once those clarifications are carefully made. There is much work to be done.

In sum, one can meet all the "basic needs" of all Americans without confusing "welfare rights" in the Catholic sense (*Pacem in Terris,* no. 11) with the political, civil, and economic rights (*Pacem in Terris,* nos. 18–22) already recognized in the U.S. Constitution and in the U.S. legal tradition. Indeed, the U.S. legal tradition already affords many ways of helping the needy and vulnerable in our midst legislatively—without a doctrine of "economic rights" in the socialist sense, but within a history of progressive social invention consistent with the American Proposition.

The "economic rights" properly so called (*Pacem in Terris,* nos. 18–22) need to be carefully distinguished from "welfare rights" (*Pacem in Terris,* no. 11). The conditional nature of the latter needs to be emphasized in order to defend human responsibility, which is the fundamental ground of human dignity. Again, the clear distinction between "economic rights" in the Catholic (and the American) sense and "economic rights" in the Marxist sense needs to be carefully drawn. Between dependency on the state and personal independence, rooted in community, there is a wide and immensely important chasm. A "synthesis" of Marxist and liberal rights is not in order. A clear distinction between the two is both necessary and urgent.

Notes

1. David Hollenbach, *Claims in Conflict: Retrieving and Renewing the Human Rights Tradition* (New York: Paulist Press, 1979), 26.
2. See Michael Novak, "Economic Rights: The Servile State," *Crisis*, October 1985, 13–14.
3. David Hollenbach, "The Growing End of an Argument," *America*, November 1985, 365.
4. Maurice Cranston, "Are There Any Human Rights?" *Daedalus* 112, 4 (Fall 1983): 7.
5. Leszek Kolakowski, "Marxism and Human Rights," *Daedalus* 112, 4 (Fall 1983): 90.
6. Ibid., 366.
7. John Courtney Murray, "Two Concepts of Government," *Theological Studies*, December 1953, 559.
8. Hollenbach, "The Growing End of an Argument," 366.
9. Novak, "Economic Rights," 9.
10. Pope John XXIII, *Pacem in Terris* (Washington, D.C.: United States Catholic Conference), no. 34.

6

The United States, Latin America, and the International Debt

Howard J. Wiarda

Latin America has been going through its worst economic depression since the 1930s. Now compounded by the international debt situation, the economic downturn the continent has experienced since the early 1980s has major implications for the United States and its foreign policy. It has not only resulted in a plummeting of the gross national product (GNP) in many countries and a lowered standard of living for many persons, but it also threatens to reverse the trend toward moderate, stable, and democratic government that has been so heartening in Latin America in the past several years. These issues of economics, politics, and their interrelations, on the international level as well as the domestic, are fraught with major consequences: for Latin America, for the United States, and for international financial and political affairs.

Into the controversy surrounding the debt issue have now stepped the U.S. Catholic bishops, with their report on *Economic Justice for All: Catholic Social Teaching and the U.S. Economy,* and the Pontifical Commission on Justice and Peace, with its more recent statement on *An Ethical Approach to the International Debt Question.* Both of these reports have many commendable and interesting things to say and one welcomes the addition of new and fresh voices to the discussion. But fresh perspectives sometimes carry dangers as well. To the extent these statements by the church are, or are perceived to be, biased, simplistic, inaccurate, or out of date, they may reflect discredit on the church instead of honor. And to the extent that they suggest wholly unrealistic or inappropriate solutions to the debt crisis, they may compound the problems of Latin America and its struggling peoples rather than provide solutions.

That is precisely the problem we face right now—and it is by no means limited to the church. The international debt has become a very "hot" issue and many groups are rushing pell-mell to offer advice and solutions. Such counsel is of course part of the democratic process of give-and-take, and to the extent it is positive and constructive it is to be welcomed. The danger at present, however, is that such advice, by its selectivity and one-sidedness, may exacerbate the crisis rather than help the several parties involved arrive at a resolution.

For the fact is that currently Latin America, the commercial banks, and the U.S. government are on a path that, though strewn with boulders and often proceeding by fits and starts, offers promise of resolving the debt crisis, or at least reducing it to manageable proportions. That is a major step forward. Yet the sometimes biased or politically motivated interventions of such agencies as the bishops or the U.S. Congress (which has recently entered the fray and is casting about for an overall solution) into this very sensitive and controversial issue may, in fact, make matters worse just at the time when the debt crisis shows promise of being resolved or may be in the process of becoming less dangerous.

It is not my purpose here to criticize the bishops' statement or the Pontifical Commission at any length. On the other hand, I do believe that in their preferential siding with the Third World, their tendency to single out the United States and the commercial banks as the causes of the problem, and their opting for an overarching "general solution" that favors one side over others, these reports are biased. Further, in a time when various partial and incremental steps are being taken that point toward a gradual lessening of the crisis rather than its "total solution," such interventions by politically motivated actors are unlikely to contribute significantly or constructively toward solving the problem. Hence, rather than a detailed critique, what follows is an alternative and perhaps more realistic statement of the background and causes of the debt crisis, its complex economic and political dimensions, and the long, slow, often lurching process of coping with it.

The Debt Issue: Background and Causes

The debt that Latin America owes to foreign creditors has the potential to be disastrous for everyone—for the banks that hold the debt, for the Latin American governments that must repay it, for the international financial system that is threatened with collapse if the debt is not paid, and for the U.S. government, which may have to face the possibility of bailing out the actors.

The sheer size of the debt is staggering: about U.S. $450 billion, with $45 million more per year being added in new interest. Brazil owes $120 billion, Mexico over $100 billion, Argentina $70 billion, and Venezuela $50 billion. On a per capita basis, Costa Rica's debt burden is the continent's heaviest.

The causes of the debt are various, but there is plenty of responsibility to go around. The private commercial banks in the 1970s were flush with petrodollars, eager to lend, and not too particular about the credit worthiness of their customers. The Latin American governments were similarly eager to borrow: for military hardware, advanced social programs, war (the Argentine case), costly consumer goods, subsidies, bloated bureaucracies, and even to feed outright corruption. The U.S. government encouraged these transactions as a way of substituting for public foreign assistance, then being diminished, and as a means of serving the foreign policy goals of stability and economic development in Latin America.

The global depression that began in 1979–80 and deepened in the following years was the precipitating factor that turned the debt "situation" into a debt "crisis." The bottom fell out of the demand for Latin America's products, markets and production dried up, and the interest rates on new loans to pay off the earlier debts soared.

Before proceeding further, it is necessary to clear up a number of myths about the debt. The first is that the debt will ever be paid back in full. It is so large that it is inconceivable that Latin America could ever pay it back. In this sense, the major agenda item in the so-called North-South dialogue, to which the writers of the bishops' and commission reports keep referring—the massive transfer of resources from North to South—has to a large extent already occurred.

Second, even though everyone knows the debt cannot be paid back, Latin America cannot be permitted to default. That would stigmatize the region as "uncivilized," make it ineligible for new loans, result in the seizure of many of Latin America's assets, and subject the area to a broad range of penalties. The costs of default to Latin America would be severe.

Third, even though the banks know these loans are uncollectible, they cannot write them off as such. If they did, not only would the management of the banks come under severe criticism from their stockholders, but some of the banks themselves with an especially high Latin American debt exposure relative to their assets might have to fold. Recognizing these dangers, most U.S. banks have moved in recent years to reduce their debt exposure, although several of the big money-market banks would still be in danger if default occurred.

Fourth, the U.S. government must help maintain the mythology that the debts are payable. The reason is that the alternatives are unthinkable. For the United States would then have to bail out the banks, come to the rescue of the Latin American governments, and also bail out the international financial system. The U.S. taxpayer would undoubtedly have to shoulder the burden of such bail-outs, a particularly unhappy prospect in this era of economic belt-tightening at home and when many of our own social assistance programs are thought to be underfunded. That is not a series of prospects that politicians or policymakers in the United States wish to face.

Hence the need, in dealing with the debt, for charades, smoke-screens, fig leaves, and dissembling. These comments are not meant to obscure the severity of the debt crisis, but they are meant to show that agendas and outcomes other than the ones the U.S. bishops and the Pontifical Commission have envisioned are operating and may be likely.

"Managing" the Crisis

But if the debt cannot be paid and default cannot be admitted, then the only possible solution is to "manage" the crisis. The question then becomes, What does managing the crisis mean?

To the banks, "managing" the debt means keeping the Latin American loans on the books as potentially collectible, even though only a trickle of interest may be coming in and no principal at all. It means continuously rolling over the debt, forgoing fees, lowering interest rates, and making new loans available—anything but admitting that the loans are no good.

To the Latin American governments, "managing" the debt means some limited belt-tightening, some compliance with International Monetary Fund-imposed austerity, and constant renegotiations over "repayment." In this way, Latin America remains "credit-worthy" but without ever paying more than a small amount of interest and never any principal.

For the United States, "managing" the debt means that no one has to face the unpalatable task of dealing with the issue squarely or bailing out either banks or Latin American governments with taxpayers' money. Moreover, in this way the United States can continue to maintain the further fiction that the debt is a purely financial matter between debtors and creditors, and not a "political" issue. For as soon as it publicly admits that the debt is political, which everyone knows it is, then the United States also must admit that it is negotiable and, essentially, uncollectible, thus letting completely off the hook some Latin American regimes that are badly in need of structural reforms to encourage greater probity and efficiency.

Hence all the parties to the debt crisis have a strong interest in maintaining the idea that it is "manageable." To do otherwise would be to admit that the debt is unpayable, that the loans cannot be collected, that the banks and Latin American governments are unsound and unstable, that the international financial system is insecure, and that the U.S. taxpayers will have to pick up the tab. Since none of these things can be admitted, the formula of "managing" the debt must be kept alive.

The strategy on the part of all the participants in the debt crisis has been to play for time, to keep postponing the day of reckoning, and to hope for the best. That is not a "great and glorious" solution to the debt crisis, but it may not be an inappropriate one, and it is probably better than most others that have been proposed.

The hope is that the world economic recovery that began in the United States in 1983 and that has by now spread to many regions of Latin America will enable these countries to *grow* out of the crisis. Since aid and assistance are always meager, economic growth is the only long-term solution. Meanwhile, Latin America under the impact of the crisis *has* begun to expand and diversify its exports, to make some structural changes, and to reform its finances and bureaucracy—all necessary changes on which observers can agree.

At the same time the private banks are rapidly converting their outstanding Latin American debt holdings to paper, selling them off at discount rates, and thus getting out from under the heavy burden of vast, uncollectible loans—while at the same time rolling up immense profits in other areas to make up for the losses they will have to absorb on their uncollectible Latin American loans. Many bankers say (though not some of the big New York banks whose loan exposure in Latin America is dangerously large) that if they are given five years, they will be out from under their Latin American loan burden. In short, the strategy is to wait the crisis out, meanwhile doing a series of small things that will attenuate the crisis and make it less severe by comparison.

If this is the strategy, how then is the debt actually *managed?* The key components have by now become familiar. They include ignoring the de-facto defaults of such comparatively small debtors as Bolivia, Ecuador, and Peru; postponing the due dates of payments; and renegotiating constantly over new "packages" of loan assistance and their repayment schedules. At the same time austerity has to be carried out by the debtor nations—some of it for real and some of it on paper only for the purpose of impressing the International Monetary Fund (IMF), which is then able to make new loans available. Meanwhile, the U.S. government also puts pressure on the private banks and the international lending agencies such as the World Bank to make additional loans available, and on the Latin American governments to carry out more reforms.

One should not underestimate the impact that austerity has had, especially on the poor, in such countries as Brazil and the Dominican Republic. There have been food riots, protests, and violent demonstrations. On the other hand, the effects have not been as bad as they are sometimes portrayed, and a number of Latin American governments have become quite adept at managing austerity just as they have managed the debt itself.

For example, the IMF has not been as draconian in the implementation of its austerity measures as its popular image would lead one to believe and it has learned how far it can go and when to back off lest the government it is pressuring actually fall. The governments of Brazil and Mexico, for instance, have been clever in imposing austerity at one time, then relaxing the rules when the protests mounted or an election was forthcoming, and then reimposing austerity once the electoral returns were in. Under the gun of an IMF mission, Mexico fired 50,000 public employees, but then rehired 30,000 of them the next week, and by the end of the year, it had found ways to put the rest—and new employees besides—back on the public payroll.

A similar process may be observed with regard to the issue of privatization. Some state-owned firms that form part of the bloated public sector in Latin America have actually been sold back into private hands. But in most cases, "privatization" has meant the "sale" of a state-owned enterprise from one public-sector corporation to another, or its consolidation into a larger state-owned economy, or its "sale" to a labor or business group that is itself part of the state system. In Argentina, not only did President Raúl Alfonsín manage these conflicting pressures brought on by the debt very cleverly; he also discovered that even austerity can be popular with voters, who are looking for greater honesty and efficiency from the government.

As a result, not a single Latin American government has taken the advice of Fidel Castro to repudiate its debts. Not even Cuba has done so. Nor has a single Latin American government yet fallen as a result of IMF-imposed austerity. Austerity's bark has so far been worse than its bite.

Furthermore, the Latin American countries are not without their own capacities to manipulate and to use the debt crisis for their own purposes. Brazilians like to say, only partially in jest, that while a little debt is a bad thing, a big debt is a good thing. Brazil's debt is so large that it holds virtually make-or-break power over the major U.S. banks and over the international financial system. Mexico has as its ace-in-the-hole a 2,000-mile border with the United States and the knowledge that Mexico is the last country in the world the United States would want to see destabilized. Most of the other Latin American countries also know that in the last analysis the United States would not allow them to "go down the tubes," that our own security interests would dictate that we would step in with a rescue package before we would allow Latin America to become unstable and thus susceptible to upheaval from which only the Soviet Union would benefit.

Seen in these lights, the debt crisis is not at all the one-way affair that is often pictured. Latin America is clearly not without finely honed skills and considerable bargaining power in dealing with the issue. Nor is this simply a case of the "colossus of the north" and its banks keeping Latin America "in chains" for their own private or strategic purposes. Though there are, of course, elements of "dependency," "asymmetry," and "injustice" involved in this issue, by themselves explanations that flow from such perspectives are surely too simple, too one-sided, too inadequate for a complete explanation. They do not at all take account of the nuance, cynicism, sophistication, and capacity for maneuver that *all* parties to the issue have demonstrated.

Toward Resolution?

Though not without its cynical as well as comic-opera aspects, the debt crisis is a very serious issue. But it is played out at several different levels, only a few of which have to do with the "great issues" of moral injustice, North-South imbalances, and ideological purity. Rather, the issue is preeminently a political issue, to be worked out by political means—all the while not admitting, at least from the U.S. viewpoint, that it is in any way a political issue.

To begin, one must distinguish between the near- and longer-term aspects of the debt crisis. In the near term, the Latin American governments and the United States have managed not altogether badly. Default and bankruptcy have been avoided; no governments have toppled; the crisis has not produced total collapse. Meanwhile the banks, the U.S. government, and the Latin American governments have all learned some lessons, the debt has been "managed," even austerity has proved survivable.

But all the steps that have been taken, while useful in the short run, probably cannot be sustained over the long term. For example, it is estimated that it will take Mexico until the year 2000 to recover from its present economic troubles. It is inconceivable that Mexico, or any other country in the region, can maintain austerity—even on the on-again, off-again basis here described—for that long a period without something fundamental giving way. In addition, while Alfonsín of Argentina, de la Madrid of Mexico, and Sarney in Brazil have all taken quite responsible positions on the debt issue, their successors might not. Waiting in the wings in all these major countries are a whole new crop of demagogic politicians who are likely to be far more radical on the debt issues than their predecessors were.

Nor can the façades and smokescreens be kept in place forever. Eventually someone will surely say, "But the emperor has no clothes on," and all the myths about the debt issue will be exploded. The issue is politically volatile as well as economically precarious, and it hangs by slender threads. If the world economic recovery proves short-lived, if the banks' stockholders demand an honest accounting, if the American taxpayer senses that he or she will be left holding the bag, if at once several Latin American governments refuse to pay—if these or any number of other possibilities should come to pass, then the entire edifice of "managing" the debt in the manner used so far could come tumbling down.

That is why many experts agree that while the strategy employed for dealing with the debt crisis has been more or less successful to this point, for the longer term a more general or comprehensive solution will have to be found. That is what the Brady modification of the Baker plan (named after the two U.S. Treasury secretaries involved) is all about.

There are three possible ways to meet the debt crisis. The first is to treat it purely as a private matter between creditors and debtors, and follow an essentially hands-off or laissez-faire policy. The second is to deal with it on an ad-hoc basis, responding to crises as they arise. The third is a general or comprehensive approach. This last solution has been advocated most often by persons who also believe in central planning, a managed economy, and the capacity of experts and technocrats to solve such problems as the debt crisis once and for all. The bishops' letter and the report of the Pontifical Commission lean toward such "total" solutions.

The administration of President Ronald Reagan was accused of following a laissez-faire approach toward the Latin American debt, but that is surely too simple a reading. The administration, for understandable political and economic reasons, much preferred to have this matter remain in the hands of the private banks and the Latin American governments, and not itself have to get involved. But it did not hesitate to step in with major U.S.-government-assisted relief packages—for Mexico in 1982 and 1987, for example—when the laissez-faire approach proved inadequate and the threat of disaster loomed.

In this way the administration combined elements of the first and second approaches, hands-off but strong involvement in times of genuine emergency. Moreover, it had very good reasons for not opting for a comprehensive solution, fearing that the issues were so complex and the debtor-country problems so infinitely varied that a general plan could well make things worse. In addition, such a "total" or overarching solution would immediately absolve the Latin American governments from ever having to make any structural reforms at all. It would also likely leave the banks—and ultimately the U.S. government and its taxpayers—holding the bag. And in the meantime, the debt crisis is on its way to being resolved: economic growth in Latin America in 1986 and 1987 (1988 was considerably less positive) was quite good for all except four countries, structural reform is going forward, and the banks have begun to get out from under the crisis.

But the administration, like the church, respects the majesty of facts and began to inch forward toward a more comprehensive solution. That is what the initial, so-called Baker plan was all about. Without ever saying he was advancing a general formula, without admitting he was moving ever so slowly toward a political solution, and still proceeding in a piecemeal fashion, Treasury Secretary James Baker nevertheless *did* take a series of political steps to resolve the issue. His pressure on the commercial banks, the World Bank, and the IMF to make additional funding available, as well as his assurances of official U.S. concern and major interventions in time of crises, did move toward a general solution. Now Secretary Baker has taken an additional step by proposing a limited system of debt forgiveness—all of which inches us closer to a more comprehensive formula while avoiding that solution's major dangers.

Conclusion

There is, in short, a great deal to be said for continuing with present policy. That policy may be interpreted as combining elements one and two, and now incorporating element three. The strategy is based on patience and prudence. It recognizes that the only solution in the long run is for Latin America to *grow* out of its economic doldrums. It shows restraint in nudging us forward toward a solution but in avoiding more comprehensive steps that may not work or that result in outright capitulation. It requires that all parties to the dispute be prepared over the long run to absorb some losses. The banks will have to absorb loss either by selling off their Latin American debt holdings at discount prices or, eventually, by writing off some Latin American loans altogether. The Latin American governments will have to absorb some pain, through austerity and the need for reform. And it is likely that the United States will similarly absorb some of the agony of the Latin American debt, either through inflation or by increased taxes. None of this will come without controversy and acrimony from all parties.

It is very likely that this is how the debt crisis will finally be "solved." The United States will generally maintain a hands-off attitude at the level of public discourse, meanwhile showing a willingness to step into genuine emergency situations, and at the same time moving all the parties slowly toward a longer-term and more general solution. Most of the banks will reduce their Latin American debt exposure over time to the point where it no longer threatens the banks' very existence. And Latin America will continue to change, to modernize, and to grow, even if this occurs on a stop-and-go basis and through a variety of crazy-quilt solutions. The debt crisis will not disappear through these means but, rather like the guerrilla threat in Guatemala, it may atrophy, become less severe, and go into what economist Albert Hirschman, in another context, called a "quasi-vanishing act."

If these scenarios prove essentially correct, then Latin America will move slowly toward a resolution of its debt crisis, and the cause of Latin American democracy will be strengthened as well. Historically, when the Latin American economies have gone under, their political systems have usually been swamped as well. But the present economic trends in the area toward recovery and renewed growth offer hope that Latin America's new and struggling democracies may be able to survive as well.

The area will still face immense economic problems that are a function of its underdevelopment; but there is evidence that gradually, incrementally, and by fits and starts, Latin America is moving toward both accelerated economic growth and a genuinely civic and democratic political culture. Moreover, a very powerful argument can be made that it is precisely such ad-hocism, gradualism, and incrementalism that are at the heart of the democratic process. Certainly such a careful strategy that proceeds slowly to "feel its way" is to be preferred to some more total and comprehensive package that is unacceptable to U.S. taxpayers or that produces in Latin America either disaster and chaos, on the one hand, or a full-fledged command economy à la Cuba or Nicaragua on the other.

It is always a delicate balancing act in Latin America among change, collapse, and survival. But in the long run as well as in the shorter term, by following the prudent, moderate, pragmatic, and incremental course here described, Latin America might just make it, both economically and politically. That course remains the most promising of the possibilities that present themselves.

7

Employment, Unemployment, and Macroeconomics

John P. Cullity

Catholics in the United States have been engaged in a remarkable dialogue in recent years. The discussions were triggered by the first draft of the Catholic bishops' Pastoral Letter on *Economic Justice for All: Catholic Social Thinking and the U.S. Economy* in late 1984 and a final draft released in late 1986.

The approved final draft of the bishops' letter continues to be read by religious leaders, legislators, businessmen, academicians, economists, and concerned members of the general public. It continues to serve as a teaching tool in thousands of churches, colleges, and schools; this study deserves careful examination.

I will here examine the letter's section on economic problems, and focus largely on its treatment of employment and unemployment issues. Before going into details, a few comments of a more general nature are needed. The composers of the bishops' letter possibly caused themselves unnecessary trouble right at the start of the discussion of economic issues, and this can be explained with a comment by a distinguished student of the relationship between religious thought and the U.S. economy. A generation ago, the late J. M. Clark of Columbia University traversed, perhaps more than anyone else, the very terrain on which the bishops are currently traveling. His collection of essays *Economic Institutions and Human Welfare* represents a standard of excellence for research in this area.[1]

In an essay dealing with free enterprise and the planned economy, Clark drew an important distinction on the role of the church
in evaluating economic problems. It is not the function of the
church, he observed, to take a position on economic questions on
which reasonable and qualified students differed. Its proper function is, rather, to take a position on economic questions in terms of
general principles that can be squared with Christian ethics, aiding
individual Christians and non-Christians to clarify their own attitudes on these matters.[2]

The bishops chose to disregard this distinction in functions. The
consequences are serious. This comment requires details. The
bishops write that their work is not a technical blueprint for
economic reform and does not provide definitive solutions. They
assert that they are simply trying to focus the light of moral
principle on some of the economic issues and choices in American
life. (This, of course, was Clark's view of the appropriate function
of a study of this sort.) They also indicate that although the
movement from principle to policy is complex and difficult, they
are willing to undertake that task. Having decided to chart this
course, they again note that moral principles themselves do not
dictate specific programs, but must interact with empirical data and
historical, social, and political realities. Further, they acknowledge
that the validity of their prudential judgments on programs depends
in part on the empirical accuracy of their information and on the
soundness of their assumptions. To be sure, they expect that on
such complex economic issues a diversity of opinions will exist,
but they also expect that statements made in the pastoral letter
about specific policies will be seriously considered by Catholics
"as they determine whether their own moral judgments are consistent with the gospel and Catholic social teaching."[3] It is clear from
these comments that the bishops consciously decided to plunge
into controversial policy issues.

Many of the differences individuals have on policy issues are the
result of differences in their moral and ethical values. Many,
however, are also based on different judgments about how the
economy actually operates, that is, on what economists like to call
"positive economics." Individuals with the same moral values can
(and often do) disagree about policy actions because they have

different perceptions about the economic consequences of the policy.

The bishops correctly point out that their prudential statements do not carry the same moral authority as their statements on universal moral principles and formal church teaching. Yet, as noted above, they urge Catholics to give serious consideration to these prudential judgments in order to determine whether or not their own moral judgments are consistent with the gospel. But this penetration into the thicket of dispute between reasonable and qualified students leaves the bishops subject to valid criticism of their own insights into positive economics. Differences on these issues inevitably dilute the effectiveness of their statements on moral principles. This is even more true if their conclusions on matters of dispute usually coincide with those of a particular side of the political spectrum.

The Bishops' Position on Full Employment

The central assumption of the statement on employment is that full employment is the foundation of a just society, but that joblessness is becoming a more widespread and deep-seated problem.[4] This has resulted from changes in the structure of the economy, which affects the quantity and quality of jobs; technological changes that have dramatically blunted employment growth in the economy's goods sector, a consequence of which could be a shift toward lower-paying and less-skilled jobs; global competition, which is costing jobs in American factories; discrimination that results in high joblessness and low pay among racial minorities and women; and high defense spending, which means a net loss of jobs because defense industries are less labor intensive. Although the U.S. economy has created more than 32 million jobs since 1970, there is a chronic and growing job shortage. Insufficient investment in certain industries and regions, inadequate education, and insufficient mechanisms to assist workers displaced by new technology have added to the unemployment problem.

We shall assess the details of this economic analysis, but let us begin with the question, When did this dismal tendency for joblessness to become more widespread and deep-rooted begin? The answer provided by the bishops' letter is not completely clear, but they seem to suggest that the chronic and growing job shortage is a recent development. For example, they state "that periods of economic recovery (from 1950 to 1980) brought unemployment rates down to the 3 to 4 percent range. Since 1979, however, the rate has generally been above 7 percent."[5]

This does not accurately summarize the effects of economic expansion on levels of unemployment rates for the 1950–80 period; the average annual unemployment rate for the six business-cycle peaks, from 1953 to 1980 was, in fact, 4.6 percent, and the range was from 2.8 percent to 7.0 percent. Nonetheless, there is general agreement that there has been a secular trend toward higher unemployment rates in recent decades. However, the question when this started is important because the economic diagnosis of a problem that started seven or eight years ago is apt to be very different than for one that began fifteen or twenty years ago.

The behavior of employment and unemployment during business recoveries deserves additional discussion. Table 7.1 shows the percentage of the working-age population with and without jobs in the sixty-fourth month of three long expansions. There is a marked upward trend in the percentage with civilian jobs, a clear decline in the percentage in the armed forces, and a substantial rise in the total percentage employed. At 62.3 percent, the March 1988 figure is higher than in any previous recovery. On the other hand, the percentage of the population that is seeking work is higher than it was in the 1960s expansion, but lower than that in the 1975–80 case.

Those who focus their attention solely on the unemployment rate are led to say the economy has grown steadily weaker, less able to absorb the unemployed. Those who look to employment as the measure of strength, on the other hand, see recoveries getting ever stronger, creating more and more jobs. What makes both these views possible is that a much larger fraction of the population is working and seeking work, rising from 61.5 percent in 1965 to 66 percent in 1988. The entry of women into the labor market has been the principal factor behind this. Moreover, since new entrants into the labor market are initially unemployed, the large number of new entrants has tended to raise the unemployment rate. This is by no means the whole story, but the main point is to show that both the employment and the unemployment figures should be considered in appraising the strength of the labor market.

TABLE 7.1
Distribution of the Working Age Population in the Sixty-Fourth Month of Three Expansion Periods
Percentage Distribution of the Population
Sixteen and Older in the 64th Month

Business Cycle Recoveries 1st 64 months	Population 16 and Older (Thous.)	Civilians Employed	Armed Forces	Total Employed	Unemployed	Total Labor Force	Not in Labor Force	Total	Unemployed (% of Total Labor Force)
11/82–3/88	185,847	61.4	0.9	62.3	3.7	66.0	34.0	100	5.5
3/75–7/80	166,391	58.3	1.3	59.6	4.8	64.4	35.6	100	7.6
2/61–6/66	131,083	56.5	2.4	58.9	2.7	61.6	38.4	100	3.9

Source: Monthly Labor Review, Bureau of Labor Statistics, U.S. Department of Labor.
Note: Recoveries beginning October 1949, May 1954, April 1958, November 1970, and July 1980 are omitted. None lasted close to 64 months. The recovery beginning in March 1975 lasted close to that and is included. Employment and unemployment data are adjusted for seasonal variations.

These facts suggest that the letter's positioning of growth in the labor force at the top of the list of causes of growing joblessness has some validity. There were sharp increases in the supply of potential workers in the 1970s. However, the Pastoral Letter's analysis seems to stress the changes in recent years, that is, from 1979. But there has been a sharp reduction in the growth rate of the nation's labor force recently. From 1970 to 1975, the civilian labor force grew 13 percent, from 1975 to 1980, it rose 14 percent; but in the next quinquennium, from 1980 to 1985, the advance was only 8 percent.

This slow pace has persisted through 1987, and projections for the remainder of the 1980s suggest continuing slow growth in the work force. The slower growth in the labor force doubtless contributed to the better performance of labor-market statistics of late. For example, the total unemployment percentage fell 5.4 percentage points from 10.8 percent at the trough of the recession in late 1982 to 5.2 percent in June 1988. This decline in the unemployment percentage was close to triple the decline recorded in average postwar recoveries. On the basis of population projections, the growth of the labor force is expected to continue declining for some time to come. This indicates grounds for greater optimism about joblessness than the letter suggests.

The bishops' letter also suggests that technological changes are causing an economic problem and job creation. It states:

> High technology and advanced automation are changing the very face of our nation's industries and occupations. In the 1970s, about 90 percent of all new jobs were in the service occupations. By 1990, service industries are expected to employ 72 percent of the labor force. Job growth in the 1980s is expected to be greatest in traditionally low-paying, high-turnover jobs in sales, clerical, janitorial, and food service. Too often these jobs do not have career ladders leading to higher skilled, higher paying jobs. Thus the changing industrial and occupational mix of the U.S. economy could result in a shift toward lower-paying and lower-skilled jobs.[6]

This somber formulation rests on the perceived effects of our shift toward a service-producing economy. However, the service-producing sector is so diverse that its jobs cannot be neatly categorized as either high-wage or low-wage. Many very low-wage workers are employed in the service sector—in fast-food restaurants, in personal-service establishments, in nursing homes. But this sector is also the home of computer services, legal services, advertising, and communications, where workers generally earn fairly high wages. There are still other branches of the service industry where wages are about average. The stereotype of jobs in the fast-growth services as low-paid and dead-end is not an accurate description of many of the jobs in this sector. According to Janet Norwood, the distinguished U.S. Commissioner of Labor Statistics, "research completed thus far shows some shift in employment toward higher paying occupations and some reduction in employment in lower paying occupations."[7]

Furthermore, an important implication for the business cycle of the takeover by the service industries is that during future recessions total employment is apt to be more stable. In the most recent recession, from July 1981 to November 1982, about 2.7 million jobs were lost. The goods-producing industries were responsible for all of this loss. The service industries, in fact, helped to stabilize total employment. This has been their typical role, but since the services' share of total employment is now far larger than it used to be, their stabilizing effect is more powerful also. This trend persists, and will be around to help reduce the severity of the next recession.

If the private-sector service industries continue to grow more rapidly than the goods-producing industries, as the Bureau of Labor Statistics projects to 1995, the trend toward smaller declines in total employment during recession is likely to continue also. Between 1984 and 1990, the bureau's "moderate growth" projection discloses an increase of 10 million in nonfarm jobs, of which 8 million are expected in the service industries, 1⅕ million in goods production, and ½ million in government. It is anticipated that between 1990 and 1995, the service industries will continue, other things being equal, to reduce the severity of recessions.[8]

The Pastoral Letter also notes with concern the disproportionately high unemployment percentage for some disadvantaged segments of our society. This should be a matter of great concern for all Americans. In 1987 the unemployment rate for teenagers was three times that of adults. Furthermore, the differential between white and black teenage unemployment rates has been widening ominously. Since the early 1970s, the overall unemployment percentage for all nonwhites has been almost consistently more than twice that of white workers. In the 1940s and early 1950s, the differences between the two groups were much smaller. In the case of male teenagers, the average ratio of the nonwhite unemployment rate to that for whites was 1.1 between 1950 and 1954. By 1960–64, it reached 1.7. During the period 1975–85 it averaged 2.4.

The heavy impact of unemployment on teenagers, and especially black teenagers, means that unemployment has been increasingly concentrated among relatively inexperienced and unskilled workers. Available statistics do not enable us to differentiate with precision between skilled and unskilled, but the unemployment percentage for those covered by unemployment insurance gives a clue to what is happening in the market for skilled labor. In recession years from 1949 to 1981, the insured unemployment percentage averaged over 5 percent. In 1982 the rate was also 5 percent. The rate in mid-1988 was 2 percent, which is about as low as it was in the 1960s boom. Meanwhile, as noted above, the unemployment percentages for teenagers and blacks have skyrocketed.

These divergent trends suggest a dual economy with persistent shortages existing side-by-side with surpluses of relatively unskilled or inexperienced workers. In a dynamic economy, shortages in some parts of the labor market frequently accompany surpluses elsewhere without becoming a matter of national concern. These become serious matters, though, when the correction of the disequilibrium comes slowly or not at all. Thus we need to devote more attention to policies that will facilitate the mutual adjustment of supply and demand in the labor markets. I cannot here evaluate the details of the call for retraining contained in the Pastoral Letter, although the need for effective training is obvious. We should be concerned, though, about the absence of any recommendation for reappraisal of other government programs that influence the efficiency of the labor market. For instance, under current provisions of the unemployment insurance program, too many individuals are tempted to work for a short time, then leave and collect unemployment insurance. More important still, there is a need to improve our understanding of the effects of minimum-wage laws on the working of our labor markets. Compassionate concern for the poor does credit to our age, and yet the programs to which it gives rise can be effective only to the degree that they meet the test of economic soundness. There is a good possibility that some of our laws do not pass this test.

The bishops' letter also reports a dramatic job loss for American workers in both manufacturing and services from increased competition in world markets. This assertion, of course, implies that reductions in imports must lead to greater spending on domestic goods. A reduction in imports may save jobs in import-competing industries, but this is likely to be matched by the less visible loss of jobs elsewhere in the economy. One measure of whether current economic policy is costing jobs is the change in total employment in the economy. By that standard, U.S. performance has been exceptional in recent years. The expansion of imports has not come at the expense of aggregate employment, as noted above. Civilian employment has grown significantly and close to 13 million more people were employed at the end of 1987 than at the end of 1982. Such a record stands in contrast to those of other developed countries, many of which are running trade surpluses but have failed to add significantly to their employment.

Throughout the ages, philosophers and religious teachers have lamented the horrors of war and searched for ways to peace. Yet their ideals have been frustrated by the course of human events. The bishops' letter laments the massive drain on the U.S. economy of the hundreds of billions spent on national defense, but unhappily we live in dangerous times, which make large national-security expenditure practically unavoidable. Nevertheless, there are always some options in a nation's foreign and military policy, and we must be alert to the opportunities that our military establishment forces us to forgo. The letter's suggestion, however, that defense spending means a net loss in the number of jobs created in the economy, because defense industries are less labor intensive, is not convincing. Periods of high defense spending have customarily been periods of low unemployment, not the opposite.

The bishops' principle solution to what they perceive to be a growing and chronic job shortage is a monetary and fiscal policy that makes full employment the number-one goal of economic policy. They also recommend that these general economic policies must also consider the menace of inflation. However, they assert that this danger must not lead to an abandonment of the full-employment goal, but to an attack on inflation directly.

To an intelligent layperson these recommendations would seem to be unexceptional. To the serious student of economic theory, it suggests that the bishops have chosen to ignore the most important debate going on in macroeconomics theory in the past fifteen years. The modern theory of rational expectations, which has recruited many of the most gifted young economic theorists in its hard-line version, asserts flatly that macroeconomic policies—more precisely, predictable macropolicies—have no effect on the real economy, that is, output and employment. In other words, the principal solution advanced in the letter will not work. The validity of the rational-expectations theory is, of course, itself subject to debate. There is, however, no excuse for totally ignoring its existence, which is what the letter does.

Specific programs and policies targeted to particular aspects of the unemployment problem are also necessary. Among the recommended cures are expansion of job-training programs in the private sector, direct job creation for structurally unemployed persons in the public sector, and other strategies such as extensive use of job sharing and a reduced workweek.

The goal of developing effective job-training programs is shared by all who have pondered with growing concern the growth of serious imbalances in the operation of our labor markets. There will, nonetheless, be differences of opinion about the efficacy of specific programs. Informed students will be skeptical about the usefulness of programs, such as a reduced workweek, to reduce the level of joblessness. Introduced in Western Europe in the early 1980s, the total ineffectiveness of programs of this type to reduce joblessness did not go unnoticed in informed circles.[9]

Some Concluding Thoughts

An acerbic critic of the bishops' letter characterized it as "a great missed opportunity."[10] Peter Berger asked pointedly whether or not it was necessary for the bishops to get into the details of policy alternatives. Wouldn't it have been more useful if they raised incisive moral questions and put them to *all* partisans? In an increasingly polarized society, religious spokespersons are in a unique position to mediate, to challenge, to civilize. But, as in labor/management relations, one cannot be a mediator and a partisan at the same time.

Another worrisome concern is the heavy emphasis the letter places on the social causes of our difficulties. There is some merit to this, but in a document that deals with moral principles there ought to be more discussion of individual responsibility. It is hard to find much discussion of this in the letter. For example, why shouldn't the bishops counsel unemployed workers of their duty to make a real search for a job, to take a reasonable job if offered, and to meet such reasonable standards as the employer may set? The responsibility to get a job and keep it is a challenge. If jobs are guaranteed to everyone whether their performance is good, bad, or indifferent, then jobs are no longer a challenge, and an important moral dimension is diminished. Individual employers, of course, also have important moral obligations with respect to their actions, which influence employment and unemployment changes and the quality of the environment in the workplace. We have an obligation to consider the moral responsibilities of union leaders, whose actions on behalf of their members may at times deny job opportunities to those outside their ranks. What are the moral obligations of cabinet members, judges, congressmen, and senators, who are often confronted with difficult moral dilemmas in considering legislation that will benefit many deserving constituents while slamming the door of opportunity shut in the faces of many others? How does one balance these moral claims? And what of those of us in the profession of economics? Have we become so bewitched by the elegance and precision of our models of market processes that we sometimes lose sight of the importance of a moral environment beyond supply and demand, the health of which is a central imperative for a humane and free society? These questions are only a few of the wide range of questions that belong on an adequate agenda of moral issues confronting individuals in our economic system. They are questions that could well be addressed by those who possess the professional moral expertise of the bishops. The bishops have boldly entered areas of partisan debate where their expertise is, to put it delicately, no greater than that of many who disagree with them. The bishops have done this at the cost of neglecting areas where their authority and expertise could be properly exercised.

Notes

1. John Maurice Clark, *Economic Institutions and Human Welfare* (New York: Alfred A. Knopf, 1967).
2. Ibid., p. 245.
3. Third draft, *Economic Justice for All,* no. 132.
4. The Pastoral Letter does not define full employment, despite the considerable stress placed on the concept. For an excellent discussion of the criteria of full employment, see Arthur F. Burns, "Economics and Our Policy of Full Employment," in *The Business Cycle in a Changing World* (New York: National Bureau of Economic Research, 1969), pp. 175–200.
5. In mid-1988, however, the jobless rate was close to 5 percent.
6. Third draft, *Economic Justice for All,* no. 142.
7. *Monthly Labor Review,* Bureau of Labor Statistics, U.S. Department of Labor (July 1985), p. 3. See also essays by Samuel M. Ehrenhall, "Taking a Look at Job Quality," *New York Times,* August 13, 1986, and Dr. Robert Samulson, "The American Job Machine," *Newsweek,* February 23, 1987, p. 57.
8. Cf. Geoffrey H. Moore, "The Service Industries and the Business Cycle," Center for International Business Cycle Research, Columbia University, January 1987.
9. Arthur F. Burns, *The United States and Germany: A Vital Partnership* (New York: Council on Foreign Relations, 1986), chap. 2.
10. Peter Berger, "Can the Bishops Help the Poor?" *Commentary* (February 1985).

8

The Rediscovery of Character: Private Virtue and Public Policy

James Q. Wilson

The most important change in how one defines the public interest that I have witnessed—and experienced—since the 1960s has been a deepening concern for the development of character in the citizenry. An obvious indication of this shift has been the rise of such social issues as abortion and school prayer. A less obvious but I think more important change has been the growing awareness that a variety of public problems can be understood—and perhaps addressed—only if they are seen as arising out of a defect in character formation.

Economics was becoming the preferred mode of policy analysis in the 1960s. In the very first issue of *The Public Interest* (1965) Daniel Patrick Moynihan hailed the triumph of macroeconomics: "Men are learning how to make an industrial economy work" as evidenced by the impressive ability of economists not only to predict economic events accurately but to control them by, for example, delivering on the promise of full employment. Months later I published an essay suggesting that poverty be dealt with by direct income transfers in the form of a negative income tax or family allowances. James Tobin made a full-scale proposal for a negative income tax and Virginia Held welcomed program planning and budgeting to Washington as a means for rationalizing the allocative decisions of government, a topic enlarged upon the following year by a leading practitioner of applied economics, William Gorham. Meanwhile, Thomas C. Schelling had published a brilliant economic analysis of organized crime, and Christopher Jencks a call for a voucher system that would allow parents to choose among public and private purveyors of education. Gordon Tullock explained the rise in crime as a consequence of individuals responding rationally to an increase in the net benefit of criminality.

There were criticisms of some of these views. Alvin L. Schorr, James C. Vadakian, and Nathan Glazer published essays in 1966, 1968, and 1969 attacking aspects of the negative income tax, and Aaron Wildavsky expressed his skepticism about program budgeting. But the criticisms themselves often accepted the economic assumptions of those being criticized. Schorr, for example, argued that the negative income tax was unworkable because it did not resolve the conflict between having a strong work incentive (and thus too small a payment to many needy individuals) and providing an adequate payment to the needy (and thus weakening the work incentive and making the total cost politically unacceptable). Schorr proposed instead a system of children's allowances and improved Social Security coverage, but he did not dissent from the view that the only thing wrong with poor people was that they did not have enough money and the conviction that they had a "right" to enough. Tobin was quick to point out that he and Schorr were on the same side, differing only in minor details.

A central assumption of economics is that "tastes" (which include what noneconomists would call values and beliefs, as well as interests) can be taken as given and are not problematic. All that is interesting in human behavior is how it changes in response to changes in the costs and benefits of alternative courses of action. All that is necessary in public policy is to arrange the incentives confronting voters, citizens, firms, bureaucrats, and politicians so that they will behave in a socially optimal way. An optimal policy involves an efficient allocation—one purchases the greatest amount of some good for a given cost, or minimizes the cost of a given amount of some good.

This view so accords with common sense in countless aspects of ordinary life that, for many purposes, its value is beyond dispute. Moreover, enough political decisions are manifestly so inefficient or rely so excessively on issuing commands (instead of arranging incentives) that very little harm and much good can be done by urging public officials to "think economically" about public policy. But over recent years this nation has come face to face with problems that do not seem to respond, or respond enough, to changes in incentives. They do not respond, it seems, because the people whose behavior we wish to change do not have the right "tastes" or discount the future too heavily. To put it plainly, they lack character. Consider four areas of public policy: schooling, welfare, public finance, and crime.

Schooling

Nothing better illustrates the changes in how we think about policy than the problem of finding ways to improve educational attainment and student conduct in the schools. As every expert on schooling knows, the massive survey of public schools that James Coleman and his associates released in 1966 found that differences in the objective inputs to such schools—pupil-teacher ratios, the number of books in the library, per-pupil expenditures, the age and quality of buildings—had no independent effect on student achievement as measured by standardized tests of verbal ability.

But as many scholars have forgotten, the Coleman Report also found that education achievement was profoundly affected by the family background and peer-group environment of the pupil. And those who did notice this finding understandably despaired of devising a program that would improve the child's family background or social environment. Soon many specialists had concluded that schools could make no difference in a child's life prospects, and so the burden of enhancing those prospects would have to fall on other measures. (To Christopher Jencks, the inability of the schools to reduce social inequality was an argument for socialism.)

Parents, of course, acted as if the Coleman Report had never been written. They sought, often at great expense, communities that had good schools, never doubting for a moment that they could tell the difference between good ones and bad ones or that this difference in school quality would make a difference in their child's education. The search for good schools in the face of evidence that there was no objective basis for that search seemed paradoxical, even irrational.

In 1979, however, Michael Rutter and his colleagues in England published a study that provided support for parental understanding by building on the neglected insights of the Coleman Report. In *Fifteen Thousand Hours,* the Rutter group reported what they learned from following a large number of children from a working-class section of inner London as they moved through a dozen nonselective schools in their community. Like Coleman before him, Rutter found that the objective features of the schools made little difference; like almost every other scholar, he found that differences in verbal intelligence at age ten were the best single predictor of educational attainment in the high school years. But unlike Coleman, he looked at differences in that attainment across schools, holding individual ability constant. Rutter found that the schools in inner London had very different effects on their pupils, not only in educational achievement but also in attendance, classroom behavior, and even delinquency. Some schools did a better job than others in teaching children and managing their behavior.

The more effective schools had two distinctive characteristics. First, they had a more balanced mix of children—that is, they contained a substantial number of children of at least average intellectual ability. By contrast, schools that were less effective had a disproportionate number of low-ability students. If you are a pupil of below average ability, you do better, both academically and behaviorally, if you attend a school with a large number of students who are somewhat abler than you. The intellectual abilities of the students, it turned out, were far more important than their ethnic or class characteristics in producing this desirable balance.

Second, the more effective schools had a distinctive ethos: an emphasis on academic achievement, the regular assignment of homework, the consistent and fair use of rewards (especially praise) to enforce generally agreed-upon standards of conduct, and energetic teacher involvement in directing classroom work. Subsequent research by others has generally confirmed the Rutter account, so much so that educational specialists are increasingly discussing what has come to be known as the "effective schools" model.

What is striking about the desirable school ethos is that it so obviously resembles what almost every developmental psychologist describes as the desirable family ethos. Parents who are warm and caring but who also use discipline in a fair and consistent manner are those parents who, other things being equal, are least likely to produce delinquent offspring. A decent family is one that instills a decent character in its children; a good school is one that takes up and continues in a constructive manner this development of character.

Teaching students with the right mix of abilities and in an atmosphere based on the appropriate classroom ethos may be easier in private than in public schools, a fact that helps explain why Coleman (joined now by Thomas Hoffer and Sally Kilgore) was able to suggest in the 1982 book *High School Achievement* that private and parochial high schools may do somewhat better than public ones in improving the vocabulary and mathematical skills of students and that his private-school advantage may be largely the result of the better behavior of children in those classrooms. In the authors' words, "achievement and discipline are intimately intertwined." Public schools that combine academic demands and high disciplinary standards produce greater educational achievement than public schools that do not. As it turns out, private and parochial schools are better able to sustain these desirable habits of work behavior—this greater display of good character—than are public ones.

Welfare

Besides the Coleman Report, another famous document appeared about that time—the Moynihan Report on the problems of the black family (officially, the U.S. Department of Labor document entitled *The Negro Family: The Case for National Action*). The storm of controversy that report elicited is well known. Despite Moynihan's efforts to keep the issue alive by publishing several essays on the welfare problem in America, the entire subject of single-parent families in particular and black families in general became an occasion for the exchange of mutual recriminations instead of a topic of scientific inquiry and policy entrepreneurship. Serious scholarly work, if it existed at all, was driven underground, and policymakers were at pains to avoid the matter except, occasionally, under the guise of "welfare reform," which meant (if you were a liberal) raising the level of benefits or (if you were a conservative) cutting them. By the end of the 1960s, almost everybody in Washington had in this sense become a conservative; welfare reform, as Moynihan remarked, was dead.

Twenty years after the Moynihan Report, Moynihan himself could deliver at Harvard a lecture in which he repeated the observations he had made in 1965, but this time to an enthusiastic audience and widespread praise in the liberal media. At the same time, Glenn C. Loury, a black economist, could observe that almost everything Moynihan had said in 1965 had proved true except in one sense—today single-parent families are twice as common as they were when Moynihan first called the matter to public attention. The very title of Loury's essay suggested how times had changed: whereas leaders once spoke of "welfare reform" as if it were a problem of finding the most cost-effective way to distribute aid to needy families, Loury was now prepared to speak of it as "The Moral Quandary of the Black Community."

Two decades that could have been devoted to thought and experimentation had been frittered away. We are no closer today than we were in 1965 to understanding why black children are usually raised by one parent rather than by two or exactly what consequences, beyond the obvious fact that such families are very likely to be poor, follow from this pattern of family life. To the extent the matter was addressed at all, it was usually done by assuming that welfare payments provided an incentive for families to dissolve. To deal with this, some people embraced the negative income tax (or as President Richard Nixon rechristened it, the Family Assistance Plan) because it would provide benefits to all poor families, broken or not, and thus remove incentive for dissolution.

There were good reasons to be somewhat skeptical of that view. If the system of payments under the program for Aid to Families of Dependent Children (AFDC) was to blame for the rise in single-parent families, why did the rise occur so dramatically among blacks but not to nearly the same extent among whites? If AFDC provided an incentive for men to beget children without assuming responsibility for supporting them, why was the illegitimacy rate rising even in states that did not require the father to be absent from the home for the family to obtain assistance? If AFDC created so perverse a set of incentives, why did these incentives have so large an effect in the 1960s and 1970s (when single-parent families were increasing by leaps and bounds) and so little, if any, effect in the 1940s and 1950s (when such families scarcely increased at all)? And if AFDC were the culprit, how is it that poor single-parent families rose in number during a decade (the 1970s) when the value of AFDC benefits in real dollars was declining?

Behavior does change with changes in incentives. The results of the negative income tax experiments certainly show that. In the Seattle and Denver experiments, the rate of family dissolution was much higher among families who received the guaranteed annual income than among similar families who did not—36 percent higher in the case of whites, 42 percent higher in the case of blacks. Men getting the cash benefits reduced their hours of work by 9 percent, women by 20 percent, and young males without families by 43 percent.

Charles Murray, whose 1984 book *Losing Ground* has done so much to focus attention on the problem of welfare, generally endorses the economic explanation for the decline of two-parent families. The evidence from the negative income tax experiments is certainly consistent with his view, and he makes a good case that the liberalization of welfare eligibility rules in the 1960s contributed to the sudden increase in the AFDC case load. But as he is the first to admit, the data do not exist to offer a fully tested explanation of the rise of single-parent families; the best he can do is to offer a mental experiment showing how young, poor men and women might rationally respond to the alternative benefits of work for a two-parent family and welfare payments for a one-parent family. He rejects the notion that character, the *Zeitgeist,* or cultural differences are necessary to an explanation. But he cannot show that young, poor men and women in fact responded to AFDC as he assumes they did, nor can he explain the racial differences in rates or the rise in case loads at a time of declining benefits. He notes an alternative explanation that cannot be ruled out: during the 1960s, a large number of persons who once thought of being on welfare as a temporary and rather embarrassing expedient came to regard it as a right that they would not be deterred from exercising. The result of that change can be measured: whereas in 1967, 63 percent of the persons eligible for AFDC were on the rolls, by 1970, 91 percent were.

In short, the character of a significant number of persons

changed. To the extent one thinks that change was fundamentally wrong, then, as Loury has put it, the change creates a moral problem. What does one do about such a moral problem? Lawrence Mead has suggested invigorating the work requirement associated with welfare, so that anyone exercising a "right" to welfare will come to understand that there is a corresponding obligation. Murray has proposed altering the incentives by increasing the difficulty of getting welfare or the shame of having it, or so as to provide positive rewards for not having children, at least out of wedlock. But nobody has yet come to grips with how one might test a way of using either obligations or incentives to alter character so that people who once thought it good to sire or bear illegitimate children will now think it wrong.

Public Finance

We have a vast and rising governmental deficit. Amid the debate about how one might best reduce that deficit (or more typically, reduce the rate of increase in it), scarcely anyone asks why we have not always had huge deficits.

If you believe that voters and politicians seek rationally to maximize their self-interest, then it would certainly be in the interest of most people to transfer wealth from future generations to present ones. If you want the federal government to provide you with some benefit and you cannot persuade other voters to pay for your benefit with higher taxes, then you should be willing to have the government borrow to pay for that benefit. Since every voter has something he or she would like from the government, each has an incentive to obtain that benefit with funds to be repaid by future generations. There are, of course, some constraints on unlimited debt financing. Accumulated debt charges from past generations must be financed by this generation, and if these charges are heavy there may well develop some apprehension about adding to them. If some units of government default on their loans, there are immediate economic consequences. But these constraints are not strong enough to inhibit more than marginally the rational desire to let one's grandchildren pay (in inflation-devalued dollars) the cost of present indulgences.

That being so, why is it that large deficits, except in wartime, have been a feature of public finance only in the past few decades? What kept voters and politicians from buying on credit heavily and continuously beginning with the first days of the republic?

James M. Buchanan, in his 1984 presidential address to the Western Economic Association, offered one explanation for this paradox. He suggested that public finance was once subject to a moral constraint—namely, that it was right to pay as you go and accumulate capital and wrong to borrow heavily and squander capital. Max Weber, of course, had earlier argued that essential to the rise of capitalism was a widely shared belief (he ascribed it to Protestantism) in the moral propriety of deferring present consumption for future benefits. Buchanan has recast this somewhat: he argues that a Victorian morality inhibited Anglo-American democracies from giving in to their selfish desire to beggar their children.

Viewed in this way, John Maynard Keynes was not simply an important economist, he was a moral revolutionary. He subjected to rational analysis the conventional restraints on deficit financing, not in order to show that debt was always good but to prove that it was not necessarily bad. Deficit financing should be judged, he argued, by its practical effect, not by its moral quality.

Buchanan is a free-market economist, and thus a member of a group not ordinarily given to explaining behavior in any terms other than the pursuit of self interest narrowly defined. This fact makes all the more significant his argument that economic analysts must understand "how morals impact on choice, and especially how an erosion of moral precepts can modify the established functioning of economic and political institutions."

A rejoinder can be made to the Buchanan explanation of deficit financing. Much of the accumulated debt is a legacy of having fought wars, a legacy that can be justified on both rational and moral grounds (Who wishes to lose a war, or to leave for one's children a Europe dominated by Hitler?). Another part of the debt exists because leaders miscalculated the true costs of desirable programs. According to projections made in 1965, Medicare was supposed to cost less than $9 billion a year in 1990; in 1985 the bill was already running in excess of $70 billion a year. Military pensions seemed the right thing to do when men were being called to service; only in retrospect is their total cost appreciated. The Reagan tax cuts were not designed to impose heavy debts on our children but to stimulate investment and economic growth; only later did it become obvious that they have contributed far more to the deficit than to economic growth. The various subsidies given to special interest groups for long seemed like a small price to pay for ensuring the support of a heterogeneous people for a distant government; no one could have foreseen their cumulative burden.

No doubt there is some truth in the proposition that our current level of debt is the result of miscalculation and good intentions gone awry. But what strengthens Buchanan's argument, I believe, is the direction of these miscalculations (if that is what they were) and the nature of these good intentions. In almost every instance, leaders proposing a new policy erred in the direction of understating rather than overstating future costs; in almost every instance, evidence of a good intention was taken to be government action rather than inaction. Whether one wishes to call it a shift in moral values or not, one must be struck by the systematic and consistent bias in how we debated public programs beginning in the 1930s but especially in the 1960s. It is hard to remember it now, but there once was a time, lasting from 1789 to well into the 1950s, when the debate over almost any new proposal was about whether it was *legitimate* for the government to do this at all. These were certainly the terms in which Social Security, civil rights, Medicare, and government regulation of business were first addressed. By the 1960s, the debate was much different: How much should we spend (not, should we spend anything at all)? How can a policy be made cost effective (not, should we have such a policy in the first place)? The character of public discourse changed and, I suspect, in ways that suggest a change in the nature of public character.

Crime

I have written more about crime than any other policy issue, and so my remarks on our changing understanding of this problem are to a large degree remarks about changes in my own way of thinking about it. On no subject have the methods of economic and policy analysis had greater or more salutary effect than on scholarly discussions of criminal justice. For purposes of designing public policies, it has proved useful to think of would-be offenders as mostly young males who compare the net benefits of crime with those of work and leisure. Such thinking, and the rather considerable body of evidence that supports it, leads us to expect that changes in the net benefits of crime affect the level of crime in society. To the extent that policymakers and criminologists have become less hostile to the idea of altering behavior by altering its consequences, progress has been made. Even if the amount by which crime is reduced by these measures is modest (as I think in a free society it will be), the pursuit of these policies conforms more fully than does the rehabilitative idea to our concept of justice—namely, that each person should receive his or her due.

But long-term changes in crime rates exceed anything that can be explained by either rational calculation or the varying proportion of young males to the population. Very little in either contemporary economics or conventional criminology equips us to understand the decline in reported crime rates during the second half of the nineteenth century and the first part of the twentieth despite rapid industralization and urbanization, a large influx of poor immigrants, the growing ethnic heterogeneity of society, and widening class cleavages. Very little in the customary language of policy analysis helps us explain why Japan should have such abnormally low crime rates despite high population densities, a history that glorifies samurai violence, a rather permissive pattern of child-rearing, the absence of deep religious convictions, and the remarkably low ratio of police officers to citizens.

In 1983 I attempted to explain the counterintuitive decline in crime during the period after the Civil War in much the same terms that David H. Bayley had used in a 1976 article dealing with crime in Japan. In both cases, distinctive cultural forces helped restrain individual self-expression. In Japan these forces subject an individual to the informal social controls of family and neighbors by making the person extremely sensitive to the good opinion of others. The controls are of long standing and have so far remained largely intact despite the individualizing tendencies of modernization. In the United States, by contrast, these cultural forces have operated only in certain periods. And when they were effective it was as a result of a herculean effort by scores of voluntary associations specially created for the purpose.

In this country as well as in England, a variety of enterprises—Sunday schools, public schools, temperance movements, religious revivals, YMCAs, the Children's Aid Society—were launched in the first half of the nineteenth century that had in common the goal of instilling a "self-activating, self-regulating, all-purpose inner control." The objects of these efforts were those young men who, freed from the restraints of family life on the farms, had moved to the boardinghouses of the cities in search of economic opportunities. We lack any reliable measure of the effect of these efforts, save one—the extraordinary reduction in the per-capita consumption of alcoholic beverages that occurred between 1830 (when the temperance efforts began in earnest) and 1850 and that persisted (despite an upturn during and just after the Civil War) for the rest of the century.

We now refer to this period as one in which "Victorian morality" took hold; the term itself, at least as now employed, reflects the condescension in which that ethos has come to be regarded. Modernity, as I have argued elsewhere, involves, at least in elite opinion, replacing the ethic of self-control with that of self-expression. Some great benefits have flowed from this change, including the liberation of youthful energies to pursue new ideas in art, music, literature, politics, and economic enterprise. But the costs are just as real, at least for those young persons who have not already acquired a decent degree of self-restraint and regard for others.

The view that crime has social and cultural as well as economic causes is scarcely new. Hardly any layperson, and only a few scholars, would deny that family and neighborhood affect individual differences in criminality. But what of it? How, as I asked in 1974, might a government remake bad families into good ones, especially if it must be done on a large scale? How might the government of a free society reshape the core values of its people and still leave them free?

They were good questions then and they remain good ones today. In 1974 there was virtually no reliable evidence that any program seeking to prevent crime by changing attitudes and values had succeeded for any large numbers of persons. In 1974 I could only urge policymakers to postpone the effort to eliminate the root causes of crime in favor of using those available policy instruments—target hardening, job training, police deployment, court sentences—that might have a marginal effect at a reasonable cost on the commission of crime. Given what we knew then and know

now, acting as if crime is the result of individuals freely choosing among competing alternatives may be the best we can do.

In retrospect, nothing I have written about crime so dismayed some criminologists as this preference for doing what is possible rather than attempting what one wishes were possible. My purpose was to substitute the experimental method for personal ideology; this effort has led some people to suspect I was really trying to substitute my ideology for theirs. Though we all have benefits that color our views, I would hope that everybody would try to keep that coloration under control by constant reference to the test of practical effect. What works?

With time and experience we have learned a bit more about what works. There are now some glimmers of hope that certain experimental projects aimed at preparing children for school and equipping parents to cope with unruly offspring may reduce the rate at which these youngsters later commit delinquent acts. Richard J. Herrenstein and I have written about these and related matters in *Crime and Human Nature*. Whether further tests and repeated experiments will confirm that these glimmers emanate from the mother lode of truth and not from fool's gold, no one can yet say. But we know how to find out. If we discover that these ideas can be made to work on a large scale (and not just in the hands of a few gifted practitioners), then we shall be able to reduce crime by, in effect, improving character.

Character and Policy

The traditional understanding of politics was that its goal was to improve the character of its citizens. The American republic was, as we know, founded on a very different understanding—that of taking human nature pretty much as it was and hoping that personal liberty could survive political action if ambition were made to counteract ambition. The distinctive nature of the American system has led many of its supporters (to say nothing of its critics) to argue that it should be indifferent to character formation. Friend and foe alike are fond of applying to government Samuel Goldwyn's response to the person who asked what message was to be found in his films: if you want to send a message, use Western Union.

Since I yield to no one in my admiration for what the founders created, I do not wish to argue the fundamental proposition. But the federal government today is very different from what it was in 1787, 1887, or even 1957. If we wish it to address the problems of family disruption, welfare dependency, crime in the streets, educational inadequacy, or even public finance properly understood, then government, by the mere fact that it defines these states of affairs as problems, acknowledges that human character is, in some degree, defective and that it intends to alter it. The local governments of village and township always understood this, of course, because they always had responsibility for shaping character. The public school movement, for example, was from the beginning chiefly aimed at moral instruction. The national government could afford to manage its affairs by letting ambition counteract ambition because what was originally at stake in national affairs—creating and maintaining a reasonably secure commercial regime—lent itself naturally to the minimal attentions of a limited government operated and restrained by the reciprocal force of mutual self-interest.

It is easier to acknowledge the necessary involvement of government in character formation than it is to prescribe how this responsibility should be carried out. The essential first step is to acknowledge that at root, in almost every area of important public concern, we are seeking to induce persons to act virtuously, whether as schoolchildren, applicants for public assistance, would-be lawbreakers, or voters and public officials. Not only is such conduct desirable in its own right, it appears now to be necessary if large improvements are to be made in those matters we consider problems: schooling, welfare, crime, and public finance.

By virtue, I mean habits of moderate action; more specifically, acting with due restraint on one's impulses, due regard for the rights of others, and reasonable concern for distant consequences. Scarcely anyone favors bad character or a lack of virtue, but it is all too easy to decide a policy of improving character by assuming that this implies a nation of moralizers delivering banal homilies to one another.

Virtue is not learned by precept, however; it is learned by the regular repetition of right actions. We are induced to do the right thing with respect to small matters, and in time we persist in doing the right thing because now we have come to take pleasure in it. By acting rightly with respect to small things, we are more likely to act rightly with respect to large ones. If this view sounds familiar, it should; it is Aristotle's. Let me now quote him directly: "We become just by the practice of just actions, self-controlled by exercising self-control."

Seen in this way, there is no conflict between economic thought and moral philosophy: the latter simply supplies a fuller statement of the uses to which the former can and should be put. We want our families and schools to induce habits of right conduct; most parents and teachers do this by arranging the incentives confronting youngsters in the ordinary aspects of their daily lives so that right action routinely occurs.

What economics neglects is the important subjective consequences of acting in accord with a proper array of incentives: people come to feel pleasure in right action and guilt in wrong action. These feelings of pleasure and pain are not mere "tastes" that policy analysts should take as given; they are the central constraints on human avarice and sloth, the very core of a decent character. A course of action cannot be evaluated simply in terms of its cost effectiveness, because the consequence of following a given course—if it is followed often enough and regularly enough— is to teach those who follow it what society thinks is right and wrong.

Conscience and character, naturally, are not enough. Rules and rewards must still be employed; indeed, given the irresistible appeal of certain courses of action—such as impoverishing future generations for the benefit of the present one—only some rather draconian rules may suffice. But for most social problems that deeply trouble us, the need is to explore, carefully and experimentally, ways of strengthening the formation of character among the very young. In the long run, the public interest depends on private virtue.

9

Does It Matter What the Bishops Said?

James Finn

Most commentators on the bishops' Pastoral Letter on the economy attempt in various ways to assess all or different aspects of their accomplishment. I intend to respond to the irreverent question posed by a number of other people: Does it matter?

Does it matter what the bishops said? To break that question down: Is anybody out there listening? Will it change to any extent the way we think, and judge, and act when we cope with economic issues? Will it influence our national policies? Or is the pastoral letter destined to join the swelling files of documents dutifully honored but gradually forgotten? Will it lend additional support to the cliché that the social teaching of the Catholic church is one of the best-kept secrets of our time?

The Pastoral Letter began its public life in a swirl of media coverage and national attention, encountering both praise and deep reservation. In response to criticism that the bishops had been far too specific in their economic and political recommendations, one of the bishops' closest advisers responded that if they had restricted themselves to the reiteration of general principles, if they had not recommended detailed and, therefore, controversial political and economic policies, no one would have paid attention to what the bishops said. He did not, of course, mean that the bishops needed or wanted attention directed to themselves, but that they did want attention directed to their teaching and that this was a most effective way to command that attention in our society.

In its way, this is a very American response. If the message gets no attention, it has no impact. The bishops and their advisers have learned this lesson well. If you boldly engage in national controversy on the level of policy, you are more likely to be noticed than if you merely offer lofty sentiments and high moral principals. The bishops now know how to command the attention of the major media in this country. The report of their deliberations is not confined to the narrower dimensions of the diocesan media that they control. They have outreach. Very shrewd. Very American. But as with the acquisition of many good things, there is a price to be paid.

Several commentators doubted whether, in making the decision to offer highly particular recommendations, the bishops had correctly assessed the risks of putting their moral authority behind what were inevitably partisan positions, based on prudential judgments that had no more authority than those with which they differed. Others pointed out that they seemed to be assuming a role more properly carried out by an educated Catholic laity that was professionally engaged in the issues that were being examined. (Some added that the existence of this large, educated laity creates a contemporary situation that is significantly different from earlier periods of American Catholic history when a relatively uneducated laity took their cues on many social questions from the more educated clergy.) Few, however, pointed out that in pursuing the course they did, the bishops might be slighting a responsibility that is undeniably theirs. The noted theologian Avery Dulles, S.J., is one of those who did.

Asserting that the bishops have a legitimate teaching role, Father Dulles also asserted that the bishops should exercise more caution in speaking out on contemporary issues and questioned whether in devoting enormous time and energy to military and economic matters they had a proper ordering of their priorities. "The impression is given that the bishops are more at ease in criticizing the performance of secular governments than in shouldering their own responsibilities." And, he continued, "Few of the American bishops today enjoy a great reputation for their mastery of theology, liturgy or spiritual direction; yet, many of them are known for their views on politics and the economy." Does this matter? "It is scarcely surprising," added Father Dulles, "if a Church which abases itself before politics and military science suffers a serious decline in conversions and in priestly and religious vocations.''[1] It matters.

The Bishops' Pins

It matters in other ways too, in both positive and negative terms, that is, in what the bishops have offered us and in what they have failed to offer us. In their Pastoral Letter the bishops have offered a number of what I have termed to myself "the bishops' pins." I have adapted the term from the story of the class in which young students were assigned subjects on which they were to write and of Billy who drew the subject of straight pins. After much troubled thought Billy completed his essay, the complete text of which read: "Straight pins are the cause of saving many lives by the not swallowing of them." The bishops' pins are those assertions that will save much intellectual confusion by the not swallowing of them. Examples are, of course, in order.

In an assertion that remained virtually unchanged through the various drafts of the letter, the bishops state that "One of the most vexing problems is that of reconciling the transnational corporations' profit orientation with the common good that they, along with governments and their multilateral agencies, are supposed to serve."[2] But without a profit orientation, such corporations could not exist, nor could the needed economic development that they do much to foster. The common good would suffer. It was, after all, not a corporate spokesman but the great labor leader Samuel Gompers who said that the greatest harm a corporation could inflict on its workers is not to make a profit. Like other entities, corporations are, of course, open to legitimate criticism when they abuse the vast power that is frequently theirs, but criticizing them for having a profit motive is like criticizing the bishops for having a religious motive.

The bishops say that "the international economic order, like many aspects of our own economy, is in crisis; the gap between rich and poor countries and between rich and poor people within countries is widening."[3] This is one area of discussion where a higher degree of particularity than the bishops offered would be welcome, for without some essential qualifications and specifications, this statement cannot be accepted as true. A number of what are termed Third World countries have lifted themselves economically so that they can no longer be termed poor. The same can be said of people within some of these countries. Further, without offering some absolute numbers the reference to the gap is seriously misleading. For example, if I have $5 and you have $10 and we both then increase our income so that I have $10 and you have $20, the gap between us will have doubled—but so will my income have doubled. In spite of the increased gap, I will be better off. The same thing applies to countries. When this is not made explicit, the reader is likely to draw the wrong conclusions.

We should also put such a grave judgment as "the international economic order . . . is in crisis" in its proper context. One student of economic growth on an international scale has concluded that "the world's recent economic history contains much to be proud of. It is probably true that for the poor people of the world the quarter century between 1950 and 1975 was the best quarter century in history. We should not forget this basic fact."[4] He also points out that the World Bank reported that during the period 1960–81 the low-income countries averaged 2.9 percent per year growth in per-capita income. What that means becomes clearer when he reminds us that during the period 1900–1950, when the United States was pulling ahead of most of the world, our per-capita growth was a little more than 1.5 percent per year.

Such comparisons should not lead us to minimize the plight of those who are poor today, nor should they allow us to be complacent about the future. But they should make us a little more hesitant to invoke the word "crisis" to describe the international economic system today. Only when we have made these essential discriminations can we move on to discuss realistically the issues of distributive justice with which the bishops are properly concerned.

The bishops also say that "the dedication of so much of the national budget to military purposes has been disastrous for the poor and vulnerable members of our own society and other societies. . . ." Let us accept this unproved statement as accurate. Does it tell us anything about how much we need to spend to provide adequately for our national defense? Might not those expenditures be necessary to defend all of our citizens, including the poor and the vulnerable? Indeed, it has been for decades the judgment of our national leaders that this is the case. Neither the concern of the bishops nor our own concern for the most needy in our society, no matter how intense, can inform our judgment about the requirements of national defense.

But are we, in fact, directing monies from our domestic services into national-defense expenditures? If so, we would expect to see the percentage of government expenditures directed to national defense going up and the percentage directed to domestic services going down. Exactly the reverse is the case. Between 1960 and 1985 the percentage of the national budget going to defense was cut almost in half, and the percentage going to domestic services almost doubled.[5] Nothing in the Pastoral Letter would have informed us of this telling finding, but it is only on this realistic basis that we can proceed to talk sensibly about the allocation of federal funds. One fundamental truth should emerge from this exercise: we cannot determine the demands of our social needs by looking at our defense budget, any more than we could determine the requirements of our national defense by looking at our social needs. The demands of these two high priorities may pull in different directions and we shall, as always, have to make choices. Compromises may well be in order. They usually are. We are likely to do better if we make them on a sound basis.

The Question of Political Will

After outlining a number of quite expensive reform measures, the bishops say that "In the end, the question is not whether the United States can provide the necessary funds to meet our social needs, but whether we have the political will to do so." This seemingly innocuous assertion is seriously misleading. It implies that we recognize our social needs, that we have the resources to deal with them, and that if we do not provide the vast funds needed it is because we lack the will to do so. This is a prevalent rhetoric in our country, but it is a rhetoric more appropriate to campaigning politicians and partisan party platforms—where it is frequently found—than to leaders who are trying to enlighten us about the relations between morality and political action.

Putting aside the question of whether the American people have "the necessary funds to meet our social needs," there is the further question of whether, in fact, we always know how to allocate funds to obtain the results we want. Some social problems have proved sufficiently intractable, and our recent past is sufficiently littered with well-funded programs that failed to resolve problems, that some measure of intellectual humility would seem to be in order. Do we, for example, know *how* to administer welfare to the needy without encouraging unneedful dependency? Are we sure that we know *how* to improve our seriously inadequate educational system? Are we confident that we know *how* to cope with a growing underclass? Have we shown that we know *how* to overcome de-facto segregation and racial discrimination? Have we made sufficient headway in overcoming drug addiction that we would know *how* to use a great infusion of additional funds? All of these issues affect the economic lives of our citizens, yet it would be difficult to give a full-throated Yes to any of these questions.

What seems to be slighted in the bishops' comment about our national will is an essential truth of Christian realism: not only is our will flawed—we *are* often weak, greedy, and selfish creatures—but so is our intellect and our imagination. Even the best intentions cannot compensate for an inadequate or misguided plan. Nor would all the funds we could muster compensate for the inadequacies of such a plan. (The bishops' substitute for the Christian realism we have a right to expect is found in their statement that "We want a world that works fairly for all." Such a world is not likely to be found this side of the Kingdom of God. Much more in the mainstream of Christian realism is John Kennedy's statement that "The world is unfair.")

But does it really matter if the bishops conclude that it is the weaknesses of our political will that is the cause of our social failures? If it implies that we have the needed resources and know how to come to the aid of the most vulnerable in our society, but simply choose not to, it does less than justice to the general good sense and generosity of the American people. More important, it seriously misleads us about the nature of our problems. It matters greatly.

The Bishops' Omissions

Does it matter if, having considered so many and such complex issues in their Pastoral Letter, the bishops then slight some few?

Or if specific spiritual direction is slighted in favor of specific economic policies? The Pastoral Letter on the U.S. economy is, after all, about how that economy affects our citizens and those of other countries. But consider the following:

The bishops correctly point out that some groups in our society suffer more cruelly from poverty than others and that among these groups children, women, and racial minorities rank high. The bishops' recommendations to alleviate poverty among these groups turn almost entirely upon changes in our social and economic structures, almost as if it were the structures that were alone the cause of poverty. But the bishops fail to bring together a number of related statistics that tell us something about why the incidence of poverty is so high among particular groups.

For example, in 1984, female-headed families constituted only 8.5 percent of the population of the United States but they made up 31.1 percent of those in poverty.[6] Further, in that 8.5 percent, minority racial groups are disproportionately represented. Over the decades, from 1960 to 1984, the percentage of births out of wedlock rose among all groups, but among blacks it made the startling increase from 17 to 52 percent. While Daniel Moynihan was once stigmatized for calling attention to such statistics, almost all analysts today agree that the increase in black families headed by single women is a major reason that the average income of black people has failed to improve as it should. With appropriate modification, the same judgment can be made about Hispanics.

These analysts also agree that those female-headed families most likely to suffer extended poverty and dependency are those headed by a teenager (or someone who was a teenager when she bore her first child). These harsh statistics take on an even more somber hue when we learn that "during the twelve-year period between 1960 and 1972, the rise in female-headed families (and teenage pregnancies) accelerated and the welfare caseload in the country quadrupled precisely at a time when unemployment had declined from what was then regarded as a high rate of 6 percent to about 4 percent."[7]

Such statistics should teach us that the economic growth and the social programs called for by the bishops—however desirable some of them might be in themselves—are inadequate to address central aspects of poverty in the United States today. An adequate program would have to consider the social behavior—including, notably, the sexual behavior—of those most likely to become mired in poverty. In her study of the current demography of poverty in the United States, Blanche Bernstein concentrated on the special problems of female-headed families. She states: "Increasingly, too, black as well as white commentators are describing teenage childbearing and out-of-wedlock births generally as a deliberate choice to live in poverty, and they are decrying that choice." Having noted that economic incentives—long considered to be the best solvent of such problems—have proved inadequate, she says that "we must consider ways to influence social behavior in order to reinforce values that lead to a more stable family life, to a better-educated society, and to greater individual discipline."[8] She does not say that this will be an easy undertaking, only that it is necessary. Yet only one sentence in the bishops' Pastoral Letter refers even obliquely to the personal responsibility of unwed teenage parents.

The bishops may have intended to avoid even the appearance of "blaming the victim," which is a laudable motive, but it does less than justice to the dignity of the poor to appear to put all the blame for their poverty on societal structures, as if poor people had no personal choice and responsibility. The *New York Times* has asserted editorially that we cannot expect to change the social, that is, the sexual, behavior of young people. The best we can do is to extend sex education and distribute contraceptives ever more liberally. (The *Times* blandly asserts this even as it reports remarkable shifts in the social behavior of people in terms of exercise, smoking, drinking, and diet, changes induced by societal pressures of various kinds.) Many others agree with that editorial judgment. All the more important, therefore, that voices of strong moral leadership should be raised against such harmful and defeatist attitudes. (It is not as if American bishops are unaware of the problem or have no recommendations to make. In November 1987 the Catholic bishops of California issued a developed statement that considered the issue of unwed, pregnant women, and in March 1989 the Pennsylvania Catholic Conference released "To Love and Be Loved," which, addressed directly to teenagers and their sexual lives, asserts the need for self-control, private virtue, and personal responsibility. But these concerns did not find their way into the Pastoral Letter.)

Does it matter that, in setting guidelines for overcoming poverty, the bishops fail to develop the importance of personal responsibility, private virtue? Since these factors are so central to Catholic social teaching, so pertinent to the incidence of poverty among particularly vulnerable groups—children, women, and racial minorities—and so clearly within the purview of the bishops' undertaking, the absence of that consideration leaves a noticeable void. It matters.

The Bishops' Voice Abroad

What the American bishops have to say about a political economy as dynamic, resilient, and innovative as our own will be heard not only within the United States, but in other countries as well. In these terms, the bishops' letter has appeared at a propitious time in modern history. In the large continent of Latin America there are encouraging trends toward democracy, less insistence on the discredited theory of dependency, greater recognition of the complexity of macroeconomics, decreasing reliance on Marxist analysis—all of which create a zone of openness to change and experimentation, and possibly a willingness to look with fewer ideological blinkers at what the political and economic structures of other countries have been able to accomplish.

Moscow's open acknowledgment that communist socialism has, after seventy years, proved itself to be an economic failure has sent tremors through the world. It has, for example, released new energies in countries of Eastern Europe, allowing their people to anticipate that they might, once again, make large economic and social decisions for themselves. The Soviet model is crumbling and in the countries of Eastern Europe both activists and analysts in the civil societies, or in the "alternative structures" as they are called, are looking for alternatives to the capitalism they once knew and the socialism they look to replace. The desperate countries of Africa are learning the bitter lesson that political ideology does not bring economic development and that if they wish to achieve such development, they must change. The countries of Asia also present a checkered pattern, but some are making remarkable economic advances and even China is experimenting with free-enterprise projects. (The cruel and bloody suppression of the peaceful calls for democracy mounted by students in Tianenman Square shows, however, that experiments in both the economic and the political order are still undependable in China.) What some of these countries are learning is that, whatever else is involved, solid economic growth will depend primarily upon the economic activism and productivity of its own citizens.

On the present international scene, the voice of the American bishops is only one and not the most important, but its reach and influence should not be underestimated. If ideas have consequences, what the bishops' letter communicates about the U.S. economy, Catholic social teaching, and the political, social, and moral values of our people will have rippling effects. Where the Pastoral Letter offers sound analyses and sensible recommendations, where it recognizes and supports those values, institutions, and policies that actually foster sound economic growth—there will it encourage the development of beneficial theory and practice in other countries. Where it fails to address significant issues, it can, obviously, offer nothing, although it may mislead by indirection. And where its understanding of the springs of economic growth is weak or skewed, and its recommendations for the distribution of economic goods are flawed, it can positively mislead those who attend closely to its teachings. At this time of great international ferment, when profound and widespread political and economic change seems more likely than it has for decades, it matters what the Catholic bishops of the United States teach about Catholic social thought and the economic order.

Having said this much, I would like to return to the caution that was voiced by Father Avery Dulles as he questioned whether or not the bishops had a proper ordering of priorities when they devoted so much attention to the immediate and pressing problems of this world and comparatively little to the spiritual order. Father Dulles did not pose a choice of either one or the other. Catholicism is an undeniably incarnational religion. It can have no commerce with an angelism that would deny our earthly passage. We are plunged into this world both materially and spiritually, and it is in this world that we must both struggle and make our way. As leaders in the church, the bishops must be concerned with both the material and the spiritual welfare of those whom they address. But there remains the question of emphasis. There can be here no definitive, abstract decision of an issue that shifts with changing circumstances. There will be times when church leaders are called to make more aggressive intervention into worldly affairs, and times when their energies and talents can best be directed elsewhere. But we should acknowledge that there is a tension here, a tension reflected not only in the activities of the church in this country and other countries but also in contemporary papal documents.

The testimony of a noted historian and religious thinker who has reflected deeply on this issue is pertinent here. Herbert Butterfield has said that meditation on the role of religion in the history of the human race should provide a tremendous background "useful to those who feel that their faith enables them to make a contribution in the realm of current affairs."[9] Later he refers to the three things that illustrate the importance of Christianity in Western civilization. And in a passage that deserves extensive quotation he writes of these three things:

> They all spring from the very nature of the Christian gospel itself, and their effects on our civilisation are merely the incidental results of the ordinary religious activity of the Church—they are not a sample or a vindication of the mundane policies of ecclesiastics. They are by-products of the missionary and spiritual work of the Church, and it is not clear that the same mundane benefits would accrue if men set out with the object of procuring the mundane benefits—if men worked with their eyes on the by-products themselves. They show that the Church has best served civilization not on the occasions when it had civilization as its conscious object, but where it was most intent on the salvation of souls and most content to leave the rest to Providence. The three things are the leavening effect of Christian charity, the assertion of the autonomy of spiritual principle, and the insistence on the spiritual character of personality. Apart from the softening effect that religion often (but perhaps not always) has had on manners and morals, these things have had their influences on the very texture of our Western civilisation.[10]

These large, even profound, judgments are applicable to our present situation. In the instance, however, the Catholic bishops have their eyes very clearly focused on the mundane benefits that they would help procure for the most vulnerable and needy in our society. However others may judge that the bishops could best expend their energies, this is the choice they have presently made. Given that choice, those of us who attend to the deliberations of the bishops should make the best use of them that we can. They have brought large issues to the concern of many who may well have neglected them. With the bishops and with other members of the Lay Commission, I believe that reflecting on the American experience in the light of Catholic teaching and on Catholic social teaching in the light of that experience should enlighten our national dialogue and debate. Within the large framework of agreement, there will be considerable disagreements, as this article itself bears witness. When such disagreements arise we should try to make them as sharp, that is, as clear and distinct as possible. Then we should continue the conversation. We are in for the long haul.

Notes

1. From an unpublished address.
2. National Conference of Catholic Bishops, *Economic Justice for All: Catholic Social Teaching and the U.S. Economy* (Washington, D.C.: USCC, 1986), no 253.
3. Ibid., no 286.
4. Arnold C. Harberger, "Economic Policy and Economic Growth," *World Economic Growth,* ed. Arnold C. Harberger (San Francisco: Institute for Contemporary Studies, 1984), 465.
5. Source: *The National Income & Product Accounts of the United States 1929–1976,* U.S. Department of Commerce, 1981. *Survey of Current Business,* July 1986, U.S. Department of Commerce. Cited in *Does America Neglect Its Poor?* by Roger A. Freeman (Stanford: Hoover Institution, 1987), appendix.
6. Blanche Bernstein, *Saving a Generation* (New York: Priority Press Publications, 1986), p. 6. A Twentieth Century Fund Paper.
7. Ibid., p. 13.
8. Ibid., p. 14.
9. Herbert Butterfield, *Writings on Christianity and History,* ed. C. T. McIntire (New York: Oxford University Press, 1979), p. 38.
10. Ibid., p. 167.

Contributors

J. BRIAN BENESTAD teaches in the Department of Theology at the University of Scranton and is the author of *The Pursuit of a Social Order: Policy Statements of the U.S. Catholic Bishops 1966–1980*.

ALLAN C. CARLSON is President of the Rockford Institute and a member of the National Commission on Children.

JOHN P. CULLITY is Professor of Economics at Rutgers University.

JAMES FINN, Editorial Director of Freedom House, is the editor of *Global Economics and Religion*.

J. PETER GRACE, Chairman of W. R. Grace and Co., directed President Ronald Reagan's Private Sector Survey on Cost Control.

MICHAEL NOVAK holds the George Frederick Jewett Chair at American Enterprise Institute and has served on the Presidential Task Force of Project Economic Justice.

WILLIAM E. SIMON, a former Secretary of the Treasury, is the Chairman of the Commission on Catholic Social Thought and the U.S. Economy.

HOWARD J. WIARDA is the author, most recently, of *Latin America at the Crossroad: Debt, Development, and the Future*.

JAMES Q. WILSON is Collins Professor of Management at UCLA and most recently co-author (with Richard Herrnstein) of *Crime and Human Nature*. His article first appeared, in slightly different form, in *The Public Interest* (Fall 1985).

Lay Commission on Catholic Social Teaching and the U.S. Economy

William E. Simon *(Chairman)*
Michael Novak *(Vice Chairman)*
Michael S. Joyce *(Assistant to Chairman)*
Patricia Leeds *(Administrative Director)*
Joseph Alibrandi
Caesar A. Arredondo
Mary Ellen Bork
Robert Buckley
Rhoda Dorsey
William Ellinghaus
Ellen Wilson Fielding
James Finn
Peter M. Flanigan
John R. Gaines
George J. Gillespie III
J. Peter Grace
Joe M. Haggar, Jr.
Alexander M. Haig
Walter J. Hickel
Edward Littlejohn
Clare Boothe Luce *(deceased)*
James J. McFadden
J. Daniel Mahoney
Heberto Martinez
Steven G. Rothmeier

137

Alberta Sbragia
Frank Shakespeare
Charles G. Tildon, Jr.
Norman Ture
Julia M. Walsh
James Q. Wilson

Index